DISCOVERING **FLAVOR**

DISCOVERING

FLAVOR

HELEN LABUN JORDAN

99: THE PRESS
San Francisco, CA
Lowell, MA
2015

FIRST EDITION

Designed by Colleen Cole

ISBN 9780988266247

Dedicated to LWM

CONTENTS

PREFACE

I realized how little I knew about flavor when I ate my first cube of rotted shark. *Hákarl*, the shark, is a traditional Icelandic delicacy—it comes in chunks about half the size of standard dice, taken from the corpse of a basking shark that has rotted in a shallow grave for several months. They're served on toothpicks. You wouldn't want to touch them. I might never have sampled it if a friend hadn't decided to hold her wedding in Iceland. I'd promised myself that I would attend the first destination wedding a friend invited me to, no matter where it took place. I expected Cancun or Tuscany. Iceland's Snaefellsnes Peninsula worked, too. My boyfriend Lawrence and I packed our bags and prepared to eat weird food then celebrate matrimony.

Run an Internet search for unusual Icelandic foods, as I did from my hotel room the day I arrived in Reykjavik, and you'll quickly turn up dozens of accounts from people who have tried—and failed—to eat *hákarl*. Chef Anthony Bourdain, who makes his living from eating strange stuff, describes *hákarl* as "the single worst, most disgusting and terrible tasting thing" he has ever eaten. Travel writer Jason Wilson flew to Iceland for the purpose of trying their traditional dishes at the *Thorrablót* festival, and he couldn't go through with it. Anonymous online trip advisors posted "for the love of God, don't try the shark," and one article about Café Loki, where I chose to order my *hákarl*, described the delicacy as reminiscent of a tramp's sock soaked in urine.

Rotted shark, while new to me, is not a new discovery for Icelanders; it's been eaten for centuries. Café Loki's ambience gave me the impression of a Reykjavik Cracker Barrel, the sort of diner one finds off any U.S. interstate, with Formica-topped tables, plastic-sheathed menus, early dinner hours and blue plate specials. If we'd been in the upper Midwest, I might have looked for some pickled pigs' feet and maybe stewed tongue; here the offerings included sheep's head jelly and dried fish with butter. Lawrence enjoyed the sheep's head jelly a great deal, scooping up the fat globules that delivered a concentrated lamb-y taste, while rejecting the mashed turnips served alongside it.

When it came time for the *hákarl*, Lawrence's pleased expression turned to one of concern for his wellbeing. It was a new look for him. Lawrence is a businessman turned respected state bureaucrat who can summon the most intensely disapproving glare in Vermont. He's shaped roughly like a barrel (possibly like a keg—his first business was brewing craft beers), his shirt pockets always hold multiple pens and scraps of paper covered in illegible notes. He's been aptly described as "the dorkiest Soprano." He smiles, too, and you can hear him laugh from three buildings away (I've heard it), but mostly he looks in control of The Situation, whatever that situation might be. The *hákarl*, though, had him looking scared. Still, we'd eaten our way through the other offerings and couldn't delay the grand finale, which smelled, as promised, like a tramp's sock soaked in urine. I went first.

The little white cubes contained a taste sensation unlike anything I'd experienced before. It's a novelty straight from *Charlie and the Chocolate Factory*. Pop one in your mouth, and you'll experience a full three-course meal a la Violet Beauregarde, but without turning into a blueberry at the end.

First is the fish course, which combines the texture of a calamari ring with the taste of dried fish. If you haven't tasted dried fish before, then I suggest finding a jar of goldfish food flakes and taking a deep whiff. Dried fish tastes the way fish food flakes smell.

Next is a burn like tossing back a shot of whiskey. Icelanders will tell you to chase *hákarl* immediately with some local whiskey, Brennivin, but that ruins the three-course sensation, so don't do it. The fish includes a simulated whiskey shot on its own.

Last comes the blue cheese, and not an immoderately strong blue cheese, either. I preferred not to dwell on what produced this flavor; I preferred instead to think of sophisticated European diners who select stilton, with perhaps some apricots or wine grapes or a drizzle of honey, as their dessert course.

Ancient Icelandic food explorers had gone far, far beyond what I would ever attempt. Then, they'd sent forward into the modern day a tiny cube that delivered three courses of flavor. I wouldn't have guessed at the possibility of such an item. I had trouble imagining how anyone might have stumbled upon it. I pictured bored medieval teenagers finding a shark corpse then daring each other to lick it. Lawrence corrected me—he'd taken the trouble to read the brochures on our visit to the Natural History Museum that afternoon, and he knew *hákarl* existed because six months of rotting was the only way to make Icelandic basking sharks non-toxic. I agreed that one thing worse than eating putrid shark flesh would be eating poisonous shark flesh. Imminent starvation does help spur new taste adventures.

Before leaving Café Loki, I stopped to check in with our waitress regarding the authenticity of our *hákarl*. I'm always suspicious about whether I'm getting food that locals eat or some bland imitation manufactured for the tourists. When I put this question to the young woman who had served us, her eyes got wide.

"I'd never eat that!" she said, as if I'd insulted her.

"Well, what about your parents? Or grandparents? Is this the same stuff they'd eat or is it ... you know, weaker?"

She wrinkled her nose. "Do you know what that *is*?" she said. "There's no 'weak' *hákarl*."

It's easy to look at modern food culture and see an irreconcilable split between gourmets who get a whole novel's worth of experience from one sip of fine Champagne or nibble of caviar and those of us who will polish off a whole bag of potato chips without thinking because 1) the bag is open and 2) it tastes good. That split exists mostly in our minds. For one thing, we're all surrounded by a world full of flavors ready for exploring and, with very rare exceptions, we all have the capacity for that exploration. We can start with the items in our kitchen right now, no caviar necessary. On the other hand, to hear some folks go on about the intricate flavors in a sliver of young, local carrot or say anything detailed about wine or agree to eat rotted shark ... well, we can be forgiven for seeing that gulf of difference opening up before us.

If you'd asked me only a few years ago, I'd have told you that I stood closer to the gourmet side of the line. I'm an avid cook. Lawrence and I have hosted an open invitation dinner party every Thursday for years now for the purpose of trying out new recipes. We've gone from Midwestern-Italian fusion cuisine (Al Capone and Tax Day) to South African (Nelson Mandela memorial) to Georgia (as an excuse to use Coca-Cola as a basic cooking ingredient). Before the serious cooking hobby, I worked for a decade in different areas of market development for food, investigating things like how to establish place-based food labeling systems and the future of artisan cheese. In graduate school, I researched survey techniques for determining customers' true food preferences. I had a brief, glorious run playing Clover the Dairy Cow, the official dairy mascot of Vermont. The *hákarl* took me by surprise. It suggested a new dimension of flavor that I'd never considered. What was this architecture of flavor where you can have multiple, separate levels within a single food? It also suggested that my knowledge of food and flavor didn't reach nearly as far as I might have liked to believe.

I was still contemplating the possibilities when Lawrence and I joined the rest of the wedding party at a remote inn perched between lava fields and the gray sea, with a 16th-century church that seated forty positioned like an outhouse a respectful distance from the back door. We naturally offered to buy a round of *hákarl* for everyone. The group didn't balk. This was, after all, a group of forty people who were willing to fly to Iceland on a bride's whim and were well into the Brennivin by the time I suggested a snack. I explained what they'd taste—that distinct architecture of three strong sensations each occurring separately from the one before. I wondered whether any other food behaved the same way. No one knew. Once the conversation of weird food got started, however, other guests had their own finds to share.

One of the bride's cousins, an enthusiastic rotted shark sampler, gave me a tip: "If you like *hákarl*, you should try Bjork. Not the singer. It's a birch liqueur. You've never had anything like it."

The day after the wedding ceremony, all the guests trooped out into the cold rain for a walk along the sea shore cliffs. The waves had dug arches and tunnels out of the rock. We shuffled carefully over rain-slicked grass to the cliff edges to observe them, then trekked along the cliff tops until they descended into a beach. There, we tumbled into a warm shack that became a steam bath the instant our sodden company entered. The proprietors sold fish chowder, hot chocolate, and waffles with thick cream. A row of liquor bottles above the cash register provided additional warmth for those who wanted something stronger than hot chocolate. There, on that shelf, emerging from the steam, I spotted the Bjork. I ordered a glass.

The snifter I received held an amber-colored liquor infused with all the fragrance of a woodland waking up in spring. I truly couldn't decipher where aroma left off and taste began. Maybe it didn't. You can't drink a woodland, not really, but the scents of the liqueur implied that I could ... and that it would be delicious. It reminded me of pipe tobacco. The flavor seemed to exist entirely in its fragrance.

Now, I was getting somewhere. Now, I didn't just have random food experiences in a foreign land; I also had my own explanations (correct or not) for what made them unique. There were the flavors composed entirely of fragrance; there were the flavors that arrived in distinct phases. It was a framework for thinking about flavor that went beyond cataloging specific foods and drinks to outlining types of flavors to explore within. I hadn't thought this much about what made flavors distinctive at home, or what made them familiar, either.

The whole Iceland episode raised two questions in my mind: When would another friend get married in a place with weird food to eat (I'd encourage Indonesia, Morocco, Tokyo and/or Hong Kong), and how *does* flavor work, anyway? The first question remains a mystery. For answering the second question, though, I have the benefit of living in Vermont, a hub of food activity. Our citizens hover always on the brink of opening a specialty food business, and we are the center of the world's most important research into cookie dough for ice cream. I don't have to travel far to find people who have thought about flavor more than I ever will, who have reviewed lots of observations about what makes one flavor experience different from another and drawn conclusions based on sample sets larger than their own dining history. I could talk to these nearby flavor experts (or seriously skilled amateurs). I could also stand to read some of the entire bookshelf of cookbooks and other food writing I've amassed over the years. And pay more attention to the food and drink around me. None of these steps would represent a major inconvenience.

I understand that I could have admitted to not knowing much about flavor, shrugged, dished myself a bowl of Ben & Jerry's ice cream, and gone on to a perfectly adequate eating life. But I was curious. I wanted a framework for flavor that would let me head off in search of new flavor experiences and to get new experience from familiar flavors. That's a common desire for people who have a starting interest in food. Even for people who don't have a starting interest in food, a desire for exploration and discovery is still there, whether it's playing with the latest technology gadget, watching athletes break records for what the human body could do before, or hearing rock and roll for the first time. The Internet is saturated with "You won't believe this…" headlines because, as a rule, we're curious to learn something new, even something entirely inane involving cats. It stands to reason, then, that we would all feel the pull of a chance for discovery in one of the most common activities of our day: eating (or drinking).

The information presented here is meant to be fun and, frankly, easy. It doesn't include extraordinary measures to become a connoisseur. At no point will any reader of this book be required to eat rotten shark. Nonetheless, I hope that some will be taken by the desire to explore a little further afield than their daily routine. From there, it's a slippery slope to a *Star Trek*-like compulsion to keep going further into the unknown. And the next thing you know, you'll be on a plane to Reykjavik. Be sure to take pictures.

A Note on Flavor and Taste:

This book uses "taste" and "flavor" interchangeably, but "flavor" is technically more correct. You have taste buds that detect five different sensations we call "tastes": sweet, sour, bitter, salty, and savory. That's a pretty limited set of sensations and not really what we mean when we talk about the overall taste of a dish. If you ask someone to taste your grandmother's top secret marinara sauce recipe, you may want them to comment on, say, whether it has enough salt, but you also want them to experience a whole lot more than that. You want them to experience the *flavor*. But, if you ask someone to please pause and experience the flavor of your marinara, you'll sound pretentious. That is why we say taste when we really mean flavor.

xiv

CHAPTER ONE

IT'S NOT ABOUT WHAT YOU LIKE . . .
IT'S ABOUT WHAT'S DIFFERENT

I HAVE A CHART that shows how arbitrary our taste preferences can be. Technically, it's a chart from the Coffee Brewing Institute describing how to brew coffee, but I'm interpreting it to mean something bigger. The chart shows three variables. I haven't read an old-fashioned three-variable chart since high school science class. Going up one side is the measure of "Strength—Solubles Concentration" (the Y-axis, I remember that much), along the bottom (X-axis, if you will) is "Extraction—Solubles Yield as Percentage," and then diagonal lines run across the grid for ratio of coffee grams to liter of water. The chart makers put a shaded "Ideal—Optimum Balance" region in the middle, then outlined other areas with other descriptions like "Weak," "Weak-bitter," "Strong," and "Underdeveloped." Even though the chart says "Ideal" in the middle, they don't mean Platonic ideal. They mean that when they recorded the reactions of people drinking coffee prepared in different ways, the most positive responses fell in that region. In America "ideal" lies in one place, in Northern Europe another (stronger), and in Scandinavia yet another (stronger still). In truth, we have no ideal coffee, only different coffees brewed for different audiences.

The coffee brewers' insight tells us, with a great deal of consumer testing to back it up, that cultural norms shape our flavor preferences. For a more dramatic example, we could look to bugs. Generally speaking, when Americans come across a thick white grub or handful of maggots we react with disgust. Crickets and mealworms have made inroads in some trendy segments of American dining society; the writhing maggots have not. In other cultures, eating certain bugs is the norm—not disgusting at all. The eating habits of the people around us shape what we like, from coffee to bugs. They shape expectations, like the fact that supermarkets will stock many rows of sugary breakfast cereals, and health food stores will have plenty of kale. These norms reflect not only *where* we live but also the fashions of the time. We take for granted the popularity of salted caramel and Greek yogurt today, while earlier generations were fully entrenched in the culinary worlds of aspic and tinned ham, or Bubble Yum gum and Tab soda.

The coffee chart shows something else too—it shows the level of attention coffee experts pay to coffee flavor. They'll carefully chart all the variables for brewing, conduct thousands of taste tests, and write out protocols for getting the brew to match drinkers' preferences in a given country. And that's just the brewing stage; it says nothing about the attention paid to finding the correct beans, roasting those beans, blending them, and managing the quality of the beans along the way. The people behind our morning coffee pay meticulous attention to a coffee's flavor. They particularly pay attention to differences between coffees. Some of these differences relate to basic quality, whether beans have spoiled or gone stale. Usually the differences are simply different, not inherently good or bad. Is this coffee stronger or less strong than the last cup? Something becomes "bad" if it's not the intended flavor, even if that flavor tastes "good" to the individual sipping it. The study of coffee's flavor isn't about what you like; it's about what's different.

It makes sense that we should evaluate flavors based on differences, not on how much a particular person enjoys each one. Flavor is *so* subjective, and our preferences change *so* much over time (if we all had the same tastes we did at age three, no one would be drinking coffee in the first place) that the yum/yuck framework of evaluation doesn't get us very far. Suppose my friend goes to a new restaurant—I ask what she thought of the dessert menu, and she turns out to be one of those people who *doesn't like chocolate*. Her answer would mean nothing to me. I could ask a friend who is a Known Enjoyer of Chocolate her opinion of the chocolate cake on the menu and still get a useless response if she prefers a sliver of dense fudgy cake with a drizzle of sauce, and I prefer a hunk of springy cake with gooey frosting. And that's just two people; imagine if you're trying to calibrate across an entire industry. You'd never communicate effectively in terms of preferences.

We have examples of how to avoid talk of preference in non-food-related life. When greeting a bride at her wedding reception, we do not say we saw a dress we liked better in the shop window—we talk about her dress' attributes (lace, tulle, beads, veils, maybe she opted for bright orange). When proud parents present their babies, we say "Oh, she has her father's eyes," not, "I don't particularly care for that shade of blue." The eyes, the tulle, the orange are all differences without necessarily a preference. Similarly, when I go to my local coffeehouse, I see descriptions like "bright acidity with berry notes" or "earthy with a cocoa finish" across a bank of different coffees—none claiming to be *better* than the others, simply different.

The coffeehouse example represents a relatively new phenomenon in American coffee, a change in the last generation. In the 1980s, familiar slogans shied away from flavor descriptors and went with variations on "it tastes good": "The best part of waking up is Folgers in your cup" or "Maxwell House, good to the last drop." A few specialty coffeehouses existed, such as Peet's Coffee and Tea (established in 1966 in Berkeley) and the original Starbucks (established in 1971 in Seattle), but at a national scale, coffee businesses didn't foster customers who would demand nuance in their coffee flavors. Researchers had developed tools for thinking critically about coffee, like the coffee brewing chart, but these tools weren't in wide circulation.[1] In the 1990s, coffee culture changed. The Specialty Coffee Association of America (SCAA), founded in 1982 as a way to set quality standards for coffee, came into its own as a force shaping the coffee business. Their 1992 conference in Seattle (the third annual) drew over 1,800 attendees. By then, Starbucks had started expanding under the new leadership of Howard Schultz. The East Coast also got in on the specialty coffee action, with the expansion of businesses like Green Mountain Coffee Roasters beyond niche shops serving their neighbors to widely distributed coffees. As these businesses grew, they broke the dominance of an earlier generation of mediocre coffee and became "standard" coffees

---

1　The Specialty Coffee Association of America paints the 1970's to 1980's as a rather dark time of coffee research dissemination. http://www.scaa.org

themselves, while hundreds of new small roasters filled in behind to cater to our specialty coffee demands.

During this shift from 1980 to today, two things happened in how we talk about coffee flavor. People working in the coffee industry developed a specific way to communicate about the characteristics of different coffees from the tree through to the final arrival in customers' cups. This language let them be precise about what they needed from suppliers and roasters for creating their coffee blends and precise when they told people selling the final product what they'd get with their beans. At the same time, marketers changed how they approached consumers, particularly the new class of coffee connoisseurs. Check one of today's coffee aficionado sites like Coffee Review, and you'll learn that this morning you could have experienced a coffee that is, "Savory sweet, intriguing, intense. Raw honey, rich musk, night-blooming flowers, blood orange, roasted cacao nib and resiny aromatic wood in aroma and cup ... [where] aromatic wood and cacao nib carry into a gently drying finish."[2] I have no idea what that actually translates into flavor-wise, but it's a lot more specific than "good to the last drop."

I assess coffee flavors as light roast or dark roast and either black or adulterated by sugar, cream, and other unwelcome additions. It's a simple worldview. At a party one summer, standing by the cooler full of beer, I confessed my coffee shortcomings to Eric Svensson. Eric is a certified coffee sensory analyst or "cupper" at Coffee Lab International in Waterbury, Vermont, just a few miles up the road from where I live.

He agreed that most people limit themselves to choosing a roast, and that, worse, many people choose dark roast.

"Mmmm," I said to him, as if I didn't prefer dark roasts. I wanted to learn more.

Just as sommeliers can tell you about the flavor profile of a wine, coffee cuppers identify the flavors in your coffee. These aren't your average folks off the street tossing around terms like "bouquet of kiwi and pomegranate." They follow a particular vocabulary developed

---

2   The Ethiopia Sidama Deri Kochoha from CQ Coffee Roasters, retrieved from http://www.coffeereview.com on 9/27/13

to ensure that when someone declares that one producer's Ethiopian Yirgacheffe coffee has a "strong citrus note," it means the same thing as when someone on the other side of the country says it and the same thing it meant when someone else used the term five years ago. Coffee people will tell you that while wine gets the most popular attention for nuanced descriptions, wine only has 150 components that influence flavor while coffee has over 800.[3] If I could identify half a dozen of the 800 I'd be happy.

Eric is a blond-haired, enthusiastic coffee cupper who always looks like he's on his way to a Saturday afternoon cookout in somebody's backyard. Several years ago he'd worked on a specialty soda company with my boyfriend Lawrence, who describes Eric's relationship with flavor profiling as "profoundly dorky, but jargon-free." Eric later disputed this fact, in the body of an email to which he had also attached a PowerPoint with the title "Organic Acids: Preparation for Matching Pairs," appearing to support the dorky claim and refute the jargon-free. When I told Eric I wanted to learn about coffee flavors, he invited me to visit him in the coffee lab for a crash course introduction.

Coffee Lab International is a low gray building that smells great. The smell comes from a co-located coffee roasting company called Vermont Artisan Coffee and Tea. I'd been in a coffee roasting shop once when it burned the beans, and ever since I'd believed that all roasting smelled acrid and tarry. Not true. The pores of Coffee Lab International exuded coffee scents with a dark sweetness that made me want to bake a dessert more than brew a cup.

Eric met me at the entryway. We entered the roasting area, which had a black and white checkerboard floor and large equipment painted bright red, as if high school shop class had received a hip makeover and better lighting.

As we walked through the roasting area, Eric explained his problem with dark roasted coffee. Roasting coffee beans (or anything) changes their flavors. Dark roasted coffee has gone past the first crack stage (beans crack or pop and expand in size) and into the second one, when oils begin to rise to the surface of the bean. At this stage, the flavors

---

3   The "coffee people" here being Vermont Artisan Coffee and Tea, http://www.vtartisan .com/coffee-library/coffee-facts accessed September 2013.

created by the roasting process become pronounced, for example more bitterness and sometimes charred or tarry notes, making it difficult to taste the flavors inherent in the original bean. Strike one. Because the flavor comes largely from the roasting, dark roast usually ends up as the final destination for old beans, stale beans, beans that don't have a whole lot of their own flavor to offer. Strike two. Often we—or at least I—conflate dark roasted coffee with strong coffee. Strong means a coffee of any roast *brewed* to be strong—on the brewing chart, the solubles concentration would be higher. If I lived in Scandinavia, where the "ideal" brew is much stronger than it is here, I'd probably show no preference for a dark roast. Learning to understand the nuances of coffee requires stripping out static like "dark roast" that cover up the flavors contained in a particular bean.

Eric and I moved from the roasting area to a bright classroom space with long wooden tables about kitchen counter height. On one table sat eleven coffee samples in which each sample contained a shallow blue bowl of whole beans, two little white bowls of ground beans, a bowl of water, and deep spoons, all laid out like place settings for a formal high tea. According to the coffee cupping primer Eric had emailed earlier that week, the beans would be roasted to the first crack and measured into 7.5-gram samples. Each sample would be ground separately, and the water would reach at least 205 degrees Fahrenheit and contain between 125-175 ppm (and no more than 250 ppm) of dissolved minerals. The actual guide went on longer than that, and even then its details fell short of the precision available from the Coffee Lab equipment. The lab's water treatment unit included four different filters to strip everything from the water then reintroduce a two-part solution that would bring the water to the ideal mineral content for brewing coffee. The water unit constantly monitors the dissolved mineral situation, and alarms go off if it leaves the 130-160 ppm range (according to Eric's records the total dissolved solids in the water the day we sampled was 148 ppm).

I had an obvious question: "Won't I just screw this all up when I brew the coffee at home anyway?"

"Yes," Eric answered solemnly. "But not as badly as my mother does."

Eric's mother, I learned, brews a full pot of coffee then sets it aside to drink from throughout the week, with every cup reheated in the microwave a dozen times until each drop is gone. Eric doesn't bring home fancy coffee blends for his mother. Even so, she still benefits from a system full of people who spend their days deep in the details of coffee flavor and 148 parts per million-ppm measurement. Their goal is to ensure a consistent coffee. They want Eric's mother to know that each time she brews her pot of coffee, the coffee beans she begins with taste the same as the ones she used *last* week. Eric may not like his mother's coffee, but he can perform the sensory analysis required to determine that the latest batch matches her preferred flavor. Here we have the "different than" evaluation and its corollary "the same as" at work. The coffee is "good" in that they haven't allowed any moldy or otherwise defective beans into the mix, but beyond that it is simply the same. And sameness requires a high level of precision.

Imagine that you're Dunkin' Donuts, and you've invested millions of dollars in developing just exactly how you want a cup of Dunkin' Donuts coffee to taste. Endless factors are going to complicate your efforts to get that flavor in every cup at every store. Perhaps you can automate the brewing to exact specifications, but you still need to manage the coffee beans that get brewed. Many factors change the beans' taste: the variety of bean, the countries from which you source them, where in the country you source, at what altitude the trees grew, how the beans were harvested, how long they sit in storage, how they're ground, how they're roasted, how they're blended ... basically, if a butterfly flaps its wings in Colombia, you've got a new coffee flavor profile. You need a way to describe the Dunkin' Donuts flavor to everyone involved in the process, starting with the people sourcing the green beans so that they know from which farms to draw, what substitutions to make when the seasons change, what to look for in an unroasted bean. That flavor description needs to hold through to the very send of the process, where the Erics of the world also learn the Dunkin' Donuts taste and check the end product to verify that it matches that taste prototype. Only then can consumers like me pull into the Dunkin' drive-through with confidence that the coffee will taste the same as at any other Dunkin' drive-through.

A boutique coffee shop, the type that might invest in that Coffee Review pick with the rich musk and night-blooming flowers, will have done their homework on flavor descriptions, too. They aren't a franchise like Dunkin'; they don't want a uniform product that tastes like the coffee shop one town over, but they still want consistency. They may have flexibility to, for example, change the coffee on offer as the harvest season changes, but they still want to know what the coffee will taste like when they serve it. If they request a particular blend from a particular source, they want it to taste the way it did the last time they ordered it. If they decide to branch out into new varieties, they will want to communicate with their supplier about how that variety should taste and be able to reasonably predict if their customers might enjoy it. They might see their coffee as "better than" Dunkin' Donuts, but the more relevant fact is that they can describe what makes their choices *different from* Dunkin' Donuts.

Before getting to the sampling table, Eric started the lesson with coffee's equivalent of a translation dictionary: a wooden box of 36 aroma vials and a book of their corresponding descriptions. Aroma makes up most of coffee's flavor; it's what saves it from being bitter water, and the officially recognized fragrances in the box included garden peas, cooked beef, balsamic rice and toast.[4] Hints of these aromas blend into the overall aroma of "coffee,"," although not all at once. Different coffees have different bouquets just like wines do. Eric passed me a vial.

"What's this?" he asked.

I sniffed. "It smells sweet," I said, "almost caramel-y, like pecan pie. Kind of the gooey parts, maybe?"

"Think of nuts."

"Pecan."

"No, walnut," he said (not even a "Close," which I think would have been more fair).

---

4   Coffee is one of many products—which include wine, chocolate, and beer—where it's easy to find lists of common aromas and tastes online, usually in the form of Flavor Wheels. For coffee, visit the Specialty Coffee Association of America site, http://www.scaa.org.

I looked at the description list—this was the scent of raw walnut, which one shouldn't confuse with the scent of roasted nuts. The roasted nut options would have been almonds, peanuts, and hazelnuts. Eric explained that it didn't matter if I got "raw walnut" on the first try—what mattered was remembering that *that smell* in the coffee lexicon meant "raw walnut." So, for me, "goo between the pecans in pecan pie" translated to "raw walnut."

After experimenting some more with raw potato, black currant, and cedar, we moved on to sniffing the actual coffee grounds. I took a deep whiff of the first sample. Then another. Then held out the bowl to my instructor. "I smell coffee."

Eric inhaled. "How about blueberries, do you smell blueberries?"

I tried again. By gosh, yes, yes I *did* smell blueberries. Same with the next sample, then the next. Suddenly all I could smell was blueberry. Eric suggested I not try so hard.

"It doesn't have to be aromas that you think of; it can just be associations, like 'that smells like Aunt Mary's house at Christmas,'" he said. He offered the hint that Sample No. 11 would smell nothing like blueberries.

I stuck my nose into Sample No. 11 and breathed in deeply with an open mind. *Images,* I coached myself, *your first thoughts, anything ...* I pictured a scene with faded colors, a 1950s pickup truck loaded with hay, bouncing along dusty summer roads, between fields in a drought. "Straw?" I guessed. "Hay?" Does straw even smell different from hay?

"Robusta," Eric identified the coffee species. "So, yeah. And hints of rubber ..." he took a less dramatic sniff, "Maybe some petroleum."

I mentally added a filling station to the scene. At the filling station, they would serve dusty tasting coffee.

Next Eric poured the 205-degree water with exactly 148 ppm of dissolved minerals into the little white bowls of coffee grounds. According to the cupping guide, this third stage in aroma identification required us to:

> Allow [the coffee] to sit until all cups are poured, then begin to break the head or foam and smell the aroma. Breaking involves placing the spoon into the cup below the crust and stirring vigorously while your

nose is directly above the cup. Inhale the aroma rising
from the grounds, rinse your spoon and move to the
next cup.[5]

I made my way around the table, stirring vigorously and poking
my nose into the steam, taking notes on scrap paper: "blueberry,"
"lemon-y blueberry," "like cooked food," "hint of soy sauce?" I had a
muddled image of people gathered around a dimly lit stove, more like
a half-remembered dream than anything tangible I could use to build
my aroma vocabulary. If I drew any conclusion from this exercise, it
was that I don't pay enough attention to what I'm smelling during the
normal course of a day. When was the last time I'd inhaled deeply of
blueberries? Had I baked a cobbler recently? Was there lemon added?

Next came sipping the coffee:

Place your spoon in the cup and draw two-thirds of a
spoonful of brew (without any grounds) and sip in the
brew with a great deal of noise and ceremony. (This
will cause you to draw the sample of coffee into your
mouth along with a large supply of air).[6]

Eric demonstrated. He could slurp coffee with great ceremony, not
to mention a loud inhalation sound that would make any yogi proud,
without getting any liquid up his nose. It requires practice. I compro-
mised by focusing in my first sip on how much noise I could make, to
show I wasn't embarrassed to slurp loudly, then taking a second, qui-
eter sip to focus on the flavor. True professionals don't compartmental-
ize their sampling in this way.

Coffee made for sensory analysis purposes doesn't taste like what
we sit down with in our mugs at home. Or, I hope it doesn't taste like
what you sit down with. It's thin to the point of being a weak tea.
According to food scientist Barbara Stuckey, who evaluates the flavors
of a wide range of products, thinning out the original substance is the
preferred method for pulling nuances from any strong food or beverage. She describes her food lab's efforts to precisely profile a fried

---

5   Coffee Industry Board of Jamaica, Coffee Cupping Program Manual, http://ciboj.org
    /pdf/CoffeeCuppingProgramManual.pdf.

6   *Ibid*

chicken flavor: "… First we put the battered and breaded fried chicken breast patty in a commercial blender with 200-degree deionized water and whirred it to smithereens … then we filtered the smooth liquid puree through cheesecloth."[7] Presumably the detection of nuance happens after you've done this trick enough times to get over the fact that you're swishing frapped chicken around in your mouth and that's weird.

To me, each coffee tasted sour, too.

"Bright," Eric corrected me. "It's the bright acidity."

I tried to channel bright things, like buttermilk and citrus. It didn't improve the experience. Again, practice might have helped. If I'd acclimated to the "bright" taste, it wouldn't have distracted me from the other flavors trying to get their way to my brain. If I could accept that this taste was "coffee" for the purposes of analysis, it might buy some sensory space to linger over subtleties like the hints of blueberry. I didn't reach that point of acceptance in my first go-around. My tasting notes break down when I reach the coffee sipping and turn into, "Blecch, blecch, blecch every region has its characteristic flavor. Blecch," then "!!!!"

The flavors weren't completely lost on me. The Yirgacheffe coffee did have strong citrus notes, along with the blueberry I'd smelled, and the dusty Robusta still managed to taste stale through all the confusing acidity. Eric commented that, while I turned my nose up at the Robusta, in other coffees a flavor very close to dust will contribute desirable earthiness and hints of cedar. The Sumatran coffee in our sample purportedly showed that sort of cedar flavor, somewhere beyond the bright sourness.

A coffee cupper's flavor vocabulary, while well beyond my own descriptive abilities, still doesn't come close to the novel's worth of copy marketers use to extol the nuances of gourmet coffees each year. Madison Avenue has its own language, Eric explained, a freelance Wild West of rogue descriptors that don't necessarily track with the real world. Marketers take poetic license to sell coffee regardless of

---

7   Barbara Stuckey, *Taste What You've Been Missing*, Free Press, 2012, p. 146.

what the official flavor might be. There is no regulation of the captions that describe a particular blend. Eric handed me a bag of beans from a small specialty roaster known for getting creative with their coffee words.

"What do you smell?"

"Whoa, peaches. That one's obvious. Did they add flavoring?"

"No," he said. "It's just the beans." He read from the flavor notes on front: "Peach syrup." He sniffed the beans himself and made a "that's really bizarre" face. "Okay, maybe in this case they're right."

The Madison Avenue-ization of coffee descriptions both helps and hurts average consumers' ability to appreciate different flavors. On one hand, this language does prompt us to look for those differences. If we had one or two coffees, without any taste-related details explaining what made them unique, many of us would never think to ask. We would stick instead to "good/bad" or maybe "light roast/dark roast." The marketing that irks the Erics of the world comes as part of a rising tide of coffee information made available to the coffee-curious public. On the other hand, when descriptions convey flavors that exist only in a marketer's imagination, they become worse than useless. It's difficult enough navigating the nuances of coffee flavor without red herring descriptions leading consumers on a futile search for hints of musk (or whatever).

While some marketing material is unreliable, we can find trustworthy sources. A quick online search will return the coffee flavor and aroma wheels that have been reviewed by panels of professional coffee cuppers and made available by organizations like the SCAA. One drawback in these wheels is that they give equal space to both common and rare aromas. An even simpler approach is to find single-source beans (all from a particular region) and pair them with descriptions of the distinctive characteristics of that region. The Ethiopian Yirgacheffe coffees, for example, are known for citrus notes and floral aroma, and often a berry undertone. Sumatran coffees tend to be earthy—some would say musty. These broad distinctions are often easier to detect than peculiar flavor notes like raw walnut.

While coffee has a lot of flavor information that's easy for the general public to find and understand, almost every food or drink has people behind the scenes trained to pay close attention to its flavor and any shifts in that flavor. Food companies will have research and development teams testing out each new product's flavor, and once the development is done, a cadre of quality control tasters will learn to test for consistency. Farmers and farm inspectors taste for the correct flavors in some farm products (in later chapters we'll see the considerations around *what* flavor they're tasting for). There are even professional, human taste testers for pet food[8].

The next chapter goes into the basic vocabulary for discussing flavor, not only coffee flavors, but any food or drink. That vocabulary, though, is only as good as our ability to pay attention to the thing that we're describing. The coffee-cuppers-in-training, sniffing coffee grounds and letting the aroma associations come to them, aren't thinking about how much they like the coffee; they're thinking about what makes that coffee different. In fact, I find it hard to believe anyone *could* like the coffee brewed for taste testing. It's a simple pledge to think, "What is this flavor?" and to seriously consider that question before thinking, "How much do I like this flavor?" That framework for food appreciation will work whether you're savoring a fresh cappuccino or a $500 bottle of scotch. Although, if you're drinking $500 scotch, you should also make sure that you like it.

---

8   See Chapter Two of Mary Roach's book *Gulp: Adventures on the Alimentary Canal* (2013)—*I'll Have the Putrescine: Why Your Pet is Not Like You*

CHAPTER TWO

BASIC VOCABULARY OF FLAVOR

WHEN I TAKE A SIP OF COFFEE in the morning, the true flavor is, in a way, noisy. Many sensations hit at the same time. All the stuff that people like Eric study happens: the molecules that make a blueberry or cedar aroma arrive in my nose, the coffee has been brewed to a particular point on the soluble/extraction/coffee-to-water-ratio chart, the beans have arrived at a certain state of freshness or staleness. But I don't normally notice. My brain says "coffee" and leaves it at that, unless something tastes wrong. If I brew the coffee too weak or grab a bag of particularly stale beans, I notice. My subconscious has catalogued all the components of what makes a coffee taste "right" to me, and my brain sounds the alarm when something strays too far from the familiar baseline. It's a very generalized (you could say lazy) version of Eric's focused brain sounding the alarm when a particular Yirgacheffe coffee strays too far from the familiar hints of blueberry the beans are supposed to exhibit. I may not get as precise as Eric in articulating how one morning's coffee differs from another morning's, but I could certainly add a few more words to my vocabulary—in coffee and pretty much all other food and drink.

I once learned that the basic vocabulary of flavor worked like this:

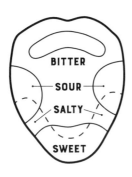

That's a tongue. The splotches represent clusters of taste buds that perceive sweet, sour, salty, and bitter, and that, collectively, create the experience of tasting food. Or so I thought. Like so many things I learned in third grade science class, the truth turns out to be more complicated.

Today, with both perfect hindsight and reference books, I can tell you that flavor has ten—not four—component parts, and most don't involve taste buds. The ones falling under taste buds' responsibility include at least five tastes, maybe more.[9] Moreover, I know that if I'd taken a closer look at my elementary school diet, I'd have found all ten. To a former fan of kid detective Encyclopedia Brown, that's disheartening news. While I spent the 1980s poring over tales of Encyclopedia Brown's adventures and wishing for an opportunity to show off my own sleuthing skills, I let that tongue chart slip by unquestioned. To add insult to injury, I could have conducted the entire investigation while enjoying my favorite snack foods.

We'll start the list of with what our taste buds sense through the direct contact with the food in our mouths.

Sweet: Cotton candy—pure sweetness.

Salty: I couldn't have been the only child who plowed through whole bags of pretzels just so she could dump the leftover salt on her tongue.

Sour: A whole sub-genre of mostly-neon candy celebrates sour. Sour Patch Kids, sour gummy worms, sour jellybeans, Tearjerkers, and Warheads are for the serious sour connoisseur.

Bitter: I tasted bitter the times I mistakenly swiped a finger lick of brownie batter before the sugar was added—unsweetened chocolate is bitter. The cruel parent trick of crushing Dramamine pills and mixing them with grape jelly to feed us before a long car trip made bitter plus gooey sweet. I had a difficult relationship with bitter as a child.

---

9 The diagram is actually wrong for more reasons than what I'm about to list. For example, all parts of your mouth have taste buds that detect the different tastes, they aren't in neat little clusters, and taste buds don't only exist in your mouth; they're found, for example, in your gut as well.

Umami: There's a surprise fifth taste with a Japanese name. To be fair, back when I was in elementary school, not many Americans talked about umami. It's a savory flavor, like you'd get in beef broth. In American snacking cuisine, ketchup has a strong umami taste.

These sensations make up what is technically "taste"—something perceived by taste buds. What we commonly call taste is really "flavor," in which the remaining four senses add depth to the food experience:

Smell: Smell provides most of a food's flavor, anywhere from 75 to 95 percent. If you don't already know smell is important, go microwave popcorn. Without that smell, what would be the point of eating this product? You can also experiment in the opposite direction by reducing smell. Coffee is nothing but bitter water with your nose plugged.

One non-intuitive element of smell is that we detect both external aromas (that popcorn smell wafting from the concession stand) and aromas from inside our mouth, traveling up into our nasal cavity through something called "retronasal olfaction." All that coffee slurping from last chapter aided in retronasal olfaction.

Touch: In food parlance we call touch "mouthfeel." Prodding your mashed potatoes with your finger will produce a touch sensation but won't do much for flavor until you put those potatoes in your mouth. The mouthfeel of mashed potatoes is one of the things that distinguishes them from a perfectly crisped french fry. That cotton candy that was pure sweetness—how do you distinguish it from other all-sugar foods? Mouthfeel.

Sight: I think of sight as candy's vocabulary. Pink means strawberry, purple grape, blue raspberry. At ten I could have told you when brown meant root beer and when it meant chocolate, or when green meant apple and when it meant lime. At the time, Dum-Dums, the miniature lollipops, had a mystery flavor that came in white, which everyone knew meant "pineapple," so it always tasted not-very-mysteriously like pineapple.[10]

Sound: After a long, hot day on the playground, there's nothing like the sound of cracking open a cold can of Orange Crush soda. After a long, hot day doing chores as a responsible adult, there's nothing like the sound of cracking open a cold beer … unless it's the sound of ice cubes in a cocktail shaker, but best to rehydrate first.

We can correlate this basic list of senses with the more complicated work of the coffee cuppers in the last chapter. Smell clearly matters; the Rosetta Stone of coffee is the aroma wheel. On the taste spectrum, sour turns out to be important—not the sour I tasted, which Eric classified as bright, but true sour, which indicates a defective bean. Mouthfeel also plays a role. I would say that coffee's "feel" is liquid of varying temperatures. The Counter Culture Coffee Flavor Wheel[11] lists the following options for the body of a coffee, in order from light to heavy: watery, tea-like, silky, slick, juicy, smooth, 2 percent milk, syrupy, round, creamy, full, velvety, big, chewy, coating. The very fact that "syrupy" is only halfway through the list tells me that I am naïve to the ranges of coffee mouthfeel. There's sight, too. The crema, that light layer on the top of espresso, holds a whole world of meaning for coffee experts (and yeah, they've got diagnostic charts for that, too).

Taste, smell, sight, sound, and touch cover how we respond to external stimuli when experiencing flavor—the molecules of the food

---

10 On April 11th, 2013, the American Chemical Society confirmed the importance of sight in flavor via a press release that included the timeless observation that many foods taste good in spite of their appearance, noting that "hashes, chilies, stews and cooked sausages have an unpleasant look, like vomit or feces." http://www.acs.org

11 This shop uses a different wheel, with more possible flavors, than the SCAA one from the previous chapter. You can find it at https://counterculturecoffee.com/tasterswheel.

connecting with taste receptors, the sound waves reaching your ears, and so on. However, that cataloguing of stimuli leaves out an important second half of the equation: what your brain does with all those signals. Your brain doesn't receive a ping from a taste bud and register "bitter," put it together with the pings of aroma, register "coffee," and move on. Instead, it wraps the experience in a whole lot of context. Coffee for waking up slowly on a Sunday morning with the paper and brunch is a different experience than *holy cow it's 3 a.m and I haven't finished my term paper, and I'm panicking and I must stay awake* coffee. Even if they're brewed exactly the same way. We can call this difference *attitude*, and it may be the most essential—and underrated—component of flavor.

We already saw attitude in the first chapter—an attitude that bugs are disgusting, or coffee should not be as strong as the Scandinavians brew it. What we believe about how a food should or shouldn't taste changes how we perceive its flavor. Cultural norms represent one sort of belief. Sometimes, belief means our brains have focused on a particular signal that may or may not prove correct, like the pineapple/mystery Dum-Dums lollipop. In one often-repeated experiment, wine tasters receive white wine dyed to look red and swear that they taste red wine. Sometimes what we expect from our food reflects ambiance, like inside a chic restaurant versus a school cafeteria. Sometimes it reflects emotions. Those emotions may be brand loyalty, like allegiance to Coca-Cola, or deeper connections, like tasting our grandmother's home cooking. All these possible feelings get lumped together into the catch-all "attitude."

A major attitude factor in flavor is familiarity. Familiarity can significantly affect our attitudes toward food. In some senses it is a variation on cultural norms. It's why you'll see American tourists scouring the streets of Tokyo to find a McDonald's amidst the fish vendors—the local cuisine may be top notch, it may even be fun to try, but for many people "strange" is not a positive food term. Within a culture's cuisine, familiarity also reflects what your family ate when you were a kid. I'm from Vermont; we had real maple syrup on our pancakes, waffles, bacon, biscuits, ice cream, oatmeal … really anything one could douse with maple syrup. We make hot sauce with it, and vodka. My family was so strict about *real* maple syrup that we turned our noses up at Grade B syrup for pancakes on account of its heavy maple flavor seeming "too close to artificial."[12] I never tasted the fake stuff until much later in life and I really, truly, deeply do not care for it. I would have a different syrup attitude had I been raised by Texans.

While the importance of familiarity makes our flavor preferences sound predetermined, in practice familiarity turns out to be easy to manufacture. A rule of thumb is that between eight and fifteen encounters with a food makes it familiar and therefore enjoyable, or at least palatable. You travel abroad and everything tastes peculiar, but then you become an ex-pat and find yourself dumping more spice in any entree than you'd ever tolerated before. You meet a boy or girl, you reach the point in a relationship of cooking for each other, his or her standard weeknight dishes aren't the ones *you* are used to, but soon enough they're a natural go-to option for Wednesday dinner. Culinary historian Bea Wilson writes that when World War II caused food shortages in Britain, preferences shifted so dramatically that as late as the 1960s one village shop selling fresh fruit hung a sign reading, "Lovely Ripe Pears—Good as Tinned!"[13]

Any food producer introducing an unusual product will have a keen interest in how to build people's familiarity with a new food. When Lawrence started the Otter Creek Brewing Company in 1989, the craft beer movement had yet to catch on in New England. Home brewers knew about a range of beer flavors, not always intentionally, but the vast beer drinking public knew Budweiser. Budweiser represented a major scientific accomplishment in controlling the components of beer flavor, producing a clean, simple beer that was (and is) bland and drinkable. Craft brews went after more interesting flavors; they played with hops, specialty malts, different yeasts, smokiness, the occasional dash of spices for a holiday beer ... back then pumpkin seemed downright reckless. If the almost-flavorless Budweiser strictly defined the "beer" flavor in most people's minds, craft brewers had some work to do to expand that definition.

---

12 For the record, though, if you're baking, making BBQ sauce, or making baked beans, Grade B is the way to go.

13 In *Swindled* (2008).

Lawrence can trace how much American flavor preferences have expanded since that time just by perusing the beers in our fridge. He pulled four of them to stage a mini-beer tasting at our kitchen table. We started with Budweiser, which had a very light, maybe a bit metallic, buttery flavor, with no aftertaste. We sampled Sierra Nevada Torpedo, a super hoppy IPA, and Arrogant Bastard Ale that I recorded as having "lingering, tannic bitter tastes with coffee notes"—I had help from Lawrence on that description. He also added that "a toasted yeasty taste gives it meaty attributes—too much of this and it will start to taste like kibble." Circling back to the light, buttery Budweiser after the other two, it now tasted like water with lackluster carbonation.

"I couldn't have sold this in New England in the '90s," Lawrence said about the Arrogant Bastard, which Stone Brewing Company did start selling in California in 1997. "But now it's at the local grocery shop for $5.99." Otter Creek's beers have become so standard that the original line might even be considered boring.

The first step in this preference shift began with encouraging customers to sample new beers. Lawrence trucked his samples to any bar or restaurant that would have him. The more people sampled, the better—not because tipsy customers are more pliable customers, but because, without realizing it, they were training themselves to think more broadly about what "beer" meant. Lawrence would ask what they usually drank, what brands they enjoyed. He knew beer very well, had tasted and paid close attention to all the varieties he could find, all around the world, and so he matched up similarities between what people knew and liked and his products. He could direct their attention as they tasted, pointing out what his beer had in common with the more familiar ones so that they focused on similarities first, differences second.

"As you build a library in your head of *what is beer*, you can wrap your head around new flavor notes and put those in context with other beers," Lawrence explained to me while I searched for the "meaty" taste in the Arrogant Bastard.

When the internal library of beer flavors changed for enough individuals, the national beer culture changed, too. Folks turning 21 today don't know how it was back in the old days.[14] Throughout the '90s, consumers started accepting more interesting ideas about what "beer" means. Some people left well enough alone and didn't bother with the craft brews. Others abandoned the bland, drinkable beers entirely. Still others landed on situational preferences, choosing the drinkable beers for something thirst-quenching and choosing more intense, complicated brews when they want to pay closer attention to their drink, perhaps taking the place of a cocktail or wine. These changes also changed the basic parameters for what counts as normal beer flavors. People searching for "weird" have to search a little further. A little smokiness or a strong hit of hops don't seem strange any more. Each shift affects the other until you end up with beers like the 1,000-IBU (International Bittering Unit) Mikeller beer, invented to be the world's most bitter beer (by comparison, a basic bitter IPA would be somewhere in the 70s or 80s),[15] and beers brewed with ingredients like oyster shells, watermelon, grape fungus, and bull testicles. That's what happens when you develop an expansive attitude towards flavor.

It's possible that salty, sweet, sour, bitter, and umami, along with smell, touch, sound, and sight and your attitude, do not explain all the mysteries of flavor. Questions remain. If it was fair to doubt the four-taste tongue diagram, it's fair to doubt this list, too. For example, what about metallic tastes? And does the burn that comes from spicy food represent mouthfeel or something else? How about the burn from alcohol? And the feeling in your mouth after drinking a very dry wine or biting into a too-green banana?[16] Nonetheless, this basic vocabulary of flavor can bring most of us a respectable distance along the path of food appreciation. It in fact brings us all the way to wine bouquets, the *sine qua non* of gourmet nuance and flavor complexity and (not coincidentally) the focus of the next chapter.

---

14 Okay, I turned 21 in 2001, so I don't know, either.

15 Lawrence would want me to point out that these are stunt beers and do not reflect the drinking preferences of a reasonable part of the population. He also doesn't think you could actually taste 1,000 IBUs. But the fact that people even bring these sorts of beers to market seems to indicate that the national palate has become much more adventurous as a whole.

16 Tannic—that's what this sensation is.

CHAPTER THREE

COMPLEX FLAVORS AND
SUBTLE FLAVOR DIFFERENCES

EVEN IN AMERICA, land of giant neon slushies and drive-through daiquiri stands, we appreciate wine. Or, many of us appreciate wine. I'm not in their ranks. I'm the person who flew to Natchitoches, Louisiana to visit the drive-through daiquiri stands. However, my fellow Americans go to tastings and classes and vineyard visits and join buying clubs in search of new wine experiences. Some go further and become connoisseurs. These wine people epitomize flavor appreciation; they get a full symphony of experience from each sip when I get the cymbals, maybe a bass drum if I focus. I will go to dinner with friends who I previously believed share my fundamental perspective on life, and someone will comment about how the wine is typical of Southern Italy or remark on a forward note of black currant. And I wonder who this person is who goes around carrying a store of flavor knowledge to which I am neither privy nor interested. And I say, "Tastes like sour grape juice," to signal my displeasure.

I don't dislike wine so much as I'm indifferent to it; it's what I'll drink if no one has offered a dry martini as an alternative. I can understand, intellectually, why so many people get so into wine. Wine, like coffee, is a complex flavor. It contains different discernible flavor notes that reveal themselves over the course of drinking. We're not talking "reveal themselves" in the sense of the hakárl's heavy-handed fish-whiskey-cheese effect. These revelations occur when, for example, the taster shifts her attention to different aspects of the wine as she sips and as the wine's chemical structure changes through its interaction with the air.[17] A complex flavor for wine means that you won't run out of new things to try, and there's always the possibility of finding something truly remarkable in the next bottle.

In some ways, wine offers an even better introduction to complex flavor than coffee because you don't have as many opportunities to mess up the flavor through mishandling the product. The greatest feat asked of the average wine drinker is to uncork the bottle. Wine's flavor changes with oxygen, so some people decant the wine to "open up" the flavor. Some wines taste better cold—light wines particularly—so some people chill them. None of these considerations matter nearly as much as coffee brewing techniques, in which, for me, the same bag of beans may go from weak tea strength one morning to dark Guinness Stout the next. Wines also travel in their own storage unit (the bottle) and should not get stale. Coffee beans get stale. Wine contains alcohol. True connoisseurs spit out the wine they sample and so remain above the effects of that alcohol, but I won't lie—I'm much more receptive to the beauties of wine after I've finished several glasses.

I never acted on wine's potential for flavor fascination until one day, soon after Lawrence and I moved in together, when I learned that he has a bottle of Italian wine labeled "Masi Campofiorin" hidden in the back of a cupboard. He had attached a "Do Not Open!!" sign to it with a rubber band. He's saving it for a special occasion. I still don't know what that occasion is. He doesn't know, either. But when that occasion arrives, I want to be damn sure that I can properly appreciate his special bottle of wine ... and learning about wine suddenly became much more relevant.

Interest in exploring wine flavors has been around since ancient times. The tombs of Egyptian pharaohs held wine containers with the date of production, region, brief description, and name of the producer. Archaeologists have uncovered evidence of wine production

---

17 You can see a simple chart of chemicals in wine and the aromas they produce (which we now know determine a great deal of the wine flavor) in Harold McGee's *On Science and Cooking*.

on pottery shards 6,000 years old.[18] In Old World Europe, wine's long-standing cultural position has developed into its own aristocracy. As Kermit Lynch writes on the first page of his *Adventures on the Wine Route*, "Just as France had its kings, noblemen, and commoners, French wine has its *grands crus, premiers crus* and there is even an official niche for the commoners, the *vins de table.*"

A long history has provided plenty of time to build up stores of arcane knowledge, rules, and traditions around wine tasting. Wine and humor writer Randall Grahm opens his helpful list of ways to know you've met a wine geek in *Been Doon So Long*:

> "If you hear one or more of the following terms, you may be in big trouble ... (a) Brix, Balling, Baumé or (steady now) Oechsle, (b) *cépage* or, even worse, *encépagement* (c) *inox*, (d) hectoliter (e) cap or tannin "management" (f) *pigeage* (g) skin contact (h) calcareous (i) *barrique* (j) maceration, *maceration* or (heaven help you) "extended" maceration (k) cold cork (l) polyphenol (m) potential alcohol (n) titratable acidity (o) *rendement* (p) authochthonous (q) *Brett* (or *Brettanomyces*) (r) "500" (s) physiological maturity (t) facultative aerobe or (u) *lieu-dit.*"

Nine additional classes of warning signals follow this set.

Some people collect wine details in the way that others collect baseball statistics. The amount of available trivia about wine suggests, indirectly, another important aspect of its appeal—emotion. You don't make room in your memory for so many details without some level of passion involved. Baseball fans care deeply about the Red Sox beating the Yankees; wine fans care deeply about opening the appropriate Champagne to celebrate the Red Sox beating the Yankees. Or perhaps they use wine to remember a summer in Provence or they anticipate what they will serve on a first date.

---

18 This fact appears in many wine histories; I happen to have taken it from the wine chapter in Harold McGee's *On Food and Cooking*.

Even for people who don't romanticize wine per se, sipping it can pull emotional strings through its connection to memory. The complexity in a wine's flavor can make it very specific—tying a particular wine to a particular time and place. Once, when a friend in the food business snuck me into a large wine trade show, I discovered a wine merchant seeking an American distributor for his South African wines. I'd studied at the University of Cape Town for a semester my junior year of college and had taken advantage of the favorable exchange rate to explore the finest wines of Stellenbosch. Years later, standing in that convention center in Boston, one sip of a Syrah from this man's winery took me straight back to South Africa, the exact pitch of its smokiness and spiciness conjuring *braais* (barbeques) and the winds off the Cape of Good Hope and one party with several members of the South African Navy that we won't go into but which involved a spit-roasted sheep and daggers. I'd had plenty of Syrahs, a few of them even from South Africa, but none had hit the exact notes of those past Stellenbosch bottles to resonate in this way. My memory knew the wine implicitly even if I couldn't articulate what made it unique.

Wine appreciation mixes our subjective emotion with very subtle flavors with technical jargon and then adds in prices that range from a few bucks to several hundred to thousands. People are bound to wonder how much of the master wine taster's art connects to any objective reality. Is it bullshit? Science corroborates some of the fabled wine bouquet—we know that wine can carry hints of different fruits because the wine and the fruit share some of the same aromatics in their chemical makeup. On the other hand, one day I read about master sommeliers identifying wine flavor by a particular acre in a particular region of Italy harvested in the sunshine of a particular year, and the next day someone else published a snarky article about a bunch of experts who couldn't tell the difference between a pricey Bordeaux and a cheap red from New Jersey in a blind tasting.[19] What, exactly, either feat has to do with how most people experience wine remains unclear.

---

19 I really did read about this; I'm not taking a cheap shot at New Jersey. Jonah Lehrer wrote about the Judgment of Princeton for the New Yorker blog in June 2012. The article is called "Does All Wine Taste the Same?"

I don't need to get into who can identify Goût de Diamants Champagne in an unmarked lineup when all I want is to pick out a few flavor notes from an $18 bottle of wine Lawrence keeps in a cupboard. Fortunately, someone has thought of tasters who share my modest expectations. When *The Essential Scratch & Sniff Guide to Becoming a Wine Expert* by Richard Betts was published in 2013, I immediately bought a copy. The Scratch and Sniff guide builds from the fact that flavor exists mostly in smell and sets aside all other distractions to focus on that component of flavor. It starts by dividing aromas into their simplest categories and builds from there. For example, if you drink red wine, you would start by distinguishing between red fruit (strawberries, raspberries) and black fruit (blueberries, blackberries). While sipping white wines you should pick up on citrus notes. Pinpointing the black fruit aspect of a red wine, while not getting me to sommelier status, would at least improve my baseline.

I decided to put Betts's work into practice by sampling wine with a few friends who I would consider enthusiastic consumers, if not professionals. I wanted them to offer commentary on what they tasted, just like Eric had provided hints for the coffee. Also, a group effort would get through more bottles of wine. Opening more bottles isn't pure hedonism. Comparing wines lets you use context to identify the flavor notes that distinguish the bottles from each other. For example, say you're interested in learning the difference between French and American oak. Setting a cabernet with a lot of French oak flavor alongside a cabernet with American oak flavor, when the two share many of the non-oak-related flavor notes, will make the French (toast, vanilla, nutmeg) and American (coconut, dill) distinctions easier to detect. Comparisons also let you know the relative strength of a flavor. Lining up a series of Syrahs that go from no smokiness up to campfire caliber helps develop a feel for the spectrum of "smoke."

Luckily, while I made my way through Betts's book, my friends Gregory and Meghan were making their way down the California coast on a vacation that revolved around tasting and purchasing wine. Surely they needed someone to help them welcome those wines to Vermont. I invited Gregory, Meghan, and their wine to join me and Lawrence and a few other friends for a sampling. We would taste a half-dozen wines, discuss, and select bottles to have with dinner. The type of friends who I mentioned at the start of the chapter, who I cut off when they want to talk wine—Gregory is one of those friends. I had come full circle. No one would eat dinner without a flavor note discussion first.

The small party gathered on a dark winter night with temperatures well below zero. I baked crackers, because homemade crackers struck me as classy and palate-cleansing. We opened the wines and set them on the mahogany table that takes up most of the space in our modest dining room.

I sampled the crackers.

I drank half a vodka martini to further cleanse my palate.

Lawrence poured his first glass of wine. He swirled the wine and breathed in the aroma matter-of-factly as if he were a doctor checking charts on a patient: get the info, process, reach a conclusion, no drawn-out pondering in between. As with the protocol for the coffee tasting, *how* you smell the wine matters. The molecules creating aroma, while invisible, are still physical things. The wine glass shapes how they reach your nose. Champagne flutes, for example, hold carbonation better but also limit how much of the fragrance you get at a sip. The old fashioned wide Champagne glasses make the bubbly less bubbly but also release more of the molecules that make up the fragrance (plus, they're essential for stacking up a pyramid of glasses into a Great Gatsby-esque Champagne fountain). In beer, drinking from the bottle (or can) significantly reduces aroma, and the glass's tint prevents the drinker from seeing the color of the beverage or observing the appearance of the foam. I would have no idea what the color or foam told me about a beer, but for people like Lawrence who know about these things, it's important. So, drinking from bottles is out, drinking from well shaped glasses is in.

I swirled my own glass of wine. Nothing spilled. I sniffed. It smelled like wine. I took a sip. It tasted sour to me. My preferred beverages land squarely in the "bitter" taste category. My cocktails approach equal parts bitters to booze. I'm unaccustomed to sour; it was the "bright" coffee problem all over again. I tried a different wine. It tasted slightly less sour, perhaps because I'd acclimated on the first wine. I went back to the first wine. Definitely not as sour-seeming.

Gregory, standing to Lawrence's left, started a discourse on agronomy in the coastal regions of California.

I went back to the second wine. Now I couldn't tell which was more sour.

Gregory moved on to explain new techniques in riddling (which, for the record, relates to sediment in Champagne, not what we were drinking).

"Scratch and sniff!" I pointed to where I'd set Betts's guide open on the table. "We're supposed to keep it at the scratch and sniff level!"

Our friend Rowan, who has written actual books about flavor, with whole chapters about wine, dutifully sniffed Betts's book.[20]

"I'm getting hints of blackberry," Meghan offered. Lawrence murmured in agreement.

Finally. Blackberry would fall under Betts's "black fruits" category for red wines, which was characteristic of Syrah, which was what we were drinking. I couldn't taste the blackberry, but at least I knew the book information lined up with what others tasted.

We moved on to another wine. "Raisin," Lawrence said.

I could taste raisin. Raisin, definitely. Sweet raisin, maybe even a little caramelized. I felt more optimistic.

Gregory reached for the red with raisin, took a sip, and spat it out—not in the proper swish and spit way, but in a sputtering, curdled milk drunk from the carton, get-this-out-of-my-mouth-now sort of way. "Something has gone wrong with that wine," he declared. "That is *not* right."

Great, the first flavor I could discern, and we'd disqualified the wine immediately. I poured myself a full-sized martini. I'd smelled wine; I'd tasted raisin; I was ready to move on with the evening.

Appreciating complex flavors comes down to the ability to detect subtle flavor differences. Unless you're a flavor savant, this ability

---

20 Specifically *The Farm Girl and the Pole Dancer: Wines Without Makeup* in *American Terroir* (2010)

develops in large part through familiarity. If I'd been born to Italian vintners, I'd know the wines of my home region inside and out without opening a single guide to wine aroma, relying instead on the familiarity I built passively over the years. It's like learning a language through immersion, absorbing it through the knowledge and practices of the people around you. If someone wanted to sponsor me on a yearlong wine country immersion experience, I would gladly go and bring back top-notch skills at detecting hints of blackberry. Instead, I was operating more at the high school Spanish class level, memorizing flavors like nouns and trying to pick up occasional flavor notes the way I might try to catch recognizable words from conversations rushing past me.

I had a tenuous hold on wine flavor, and I'd missed my opportunity to be born into a wine-loving environment, but that still didn't preclude me from having more than a passing familiarity with *other* food categories. After the limited success of my first wine tasting, I needed to restore my confidence in my flavor detection skills with something I'd grown up with, something ingrained in American food culture—in other words, a flavor more in the "native language" category. I chose breakfast cereal.

The American public hasn't embraced breakfast cereal as a dish of subtle nuance, but cereal in fact offers a prime example of America's most familiar food subtlety: the difference of brands. Cereal may not be a complex flavor, unfurling slowly to reveal new facets of its character over time, but it's a complicated one. Teams of food developers work many hours to invent just the right flavor profile for our Frosted Flakes and Golden Grahams. They keep the final formula under close guard so that no one else can replicate it. We the consumers then build flavor memories around our favorite products. It may not be breakfast cereals; maybe you know hamburgers or candy bars or soda pop, maybe you've been raised on the generic side of the aisle and know the generic brand identities (yes, the branded generic is a paradox). Most people have some food company whose product they've eaten in quantity over many years. Thanks to quality control done by people like Eric at the Coffee Lab, the exact flavor profile of that food may never have changed during all that time.

I divide my breakfast cereal eating life into two phases: the brand name years (when my mother did the grocery shopping) and the generic years (when I began to foot my own grocery bill). When I was a kid, my mother always insisted I wouldn't be able to tell the difference between brands advertised during Saturday cartoons and their generic equivalent. I, in turn, insisted on throwing a tantrum that ended in a brand-name purchase. Now, as an adult and a generic buyer myself, I could test her theory with a more open mind.

I sat down one afternoon a few days after the wine tasting with a bowl of Cheerios and a bowl of Generic-Os (not their real name) to test the flavor subtleties. This comparison would truly put my powers of perception to the test. It seems as though not much could be simpler than replicating a ring of whole grain oats with a light flavor that falls somewhere between toast and nothing. Lawrence walked past the kitchen table and gave the bowls a skeptical glance.

"Looks like they came out of the same factory," he said. I could have said the same about his glasses of red wine. I'd disqualified him from this experiment on the grounds that he didn't eat breakfast and so lacked the required cereal expertise. I reminded him of these facts and poured the milk.

Here is the most significant taste test result: my mother was wrong. The Cheerios held up better to the first flush of milk, and over a longer period of milk exposure, they contracted in on themselves, while the Generic-Os got unpleasantly soft all the way through, like dog kibble that had fallen into the water dish. The ability to pick out "hints of blackberry" in wine sounded more elegant, but these differences in texture were an important part of the food experience. What little taste the Generics began with dissolved as the cereal dissolved.

Food scientist Barb Stuckey confirms that I should detect a difference. She writes in *Taste*, "We frequently get requests from clients to 'knock off Heinz ketchup' or 'create an Oreo cookie clone.' [...] These projects are virtually impossible ... We want to believe that there is a magic black box into which you can feed anything—a wine, a pharmaceutical, a voice, a tomato-based condiment—and it will spit out the complete instructions for how to re-create the product. Because you can do this type of matching with paint chips, people assume it must be possible with food."[21] It isn't. There are too many factors involved. The true goal isn't to create a clone of the original product—it's to create something that's different but liked equally as well.

Cereal makers put out their product, promote their product, and hope that customers will then purchase and eat enough of their product to build a loyalty. Once you've downed enough bowlfuls, the flavor nuances become something of a second nature—like the subconscious check that my morning coffee tastes "right." Kellogg's designed Cocoa Krispies to turn the *milk* into chocolate milk, while the cereal Cocoa Puffs simply trades on being itself chocolate. If a kid eats a bowlful of Cocoa Krispies every morning, and one morning that bowl left milk unchocolated, she'll know it's gone off. Similarly, I could have drunk dozens of bottles of the same wine and when one bottle showed up tasting raisin-y, I would have known that something had gone wrong without Gregory announcing it. I could also shift my attention slightly, from all the components that make up a particular wine or particular cereal, to focus instead on a particular flavor note. I could know raisin when I tasted it like I might know raw walnut when smelling it. I'd confirmed with the cereal test that I had the ability to detect subtle differences, now I just had to apply it efficiently to my wine vocabulary. I was back to the Betts-style red fruit-black fruit—but with more optimism.

I built my wine familiarity in baby steps for a few months, drinking from whatever glass Lawrence might pour himself with dinner and then quizzing him about what I was tasting. I added "black cherry," "jam," and a more subtle variation of "raisin" to my repertoire that way. I got "green apple" in white wine. At a restaurant one night I identified "licorice" in a bottle of Zinfandel without any assistance. I topped off everyone's glass as a victory lap. My confidence was sufficiently revived for another round of wine tasting. I called Rowan back to the task of taking me through the flavors of a panel of wines. He'd written about wine; presumably he could explain it in person, too.

---

21 *Taste What You've Been Missing* pg. 145—also the source of the diluted chicken sandwich.

This time, I selected my wines from the closest liquor store. I knew I wanted to compare single attributes, so I got an unoaked Merlot and a regular Merlot that the liquor store cashier assured me had strong oak in it (not true, as it turned out). I bought a cheap Bordeaux because its description was longer than the other featured wines, claiming "aromas of ripe fruit (black currants, Morello cherries) and hints of candied violet and liquorice. The palate is generous, rich and full-flavored, long finish with hints of pepper and liquorice." Also, the label said it was purple. We had an unopened bottle of Gregory's wine left over from the first tasting, a Pinot Noir. I figured his could represent the vast realm of wines that cost more than $10 a bottle.

I put the paper bag of new wines on the kitchen table. I wasn't in hostess mode anymore, so I'd traded in the dining room, with its polished table and its pink draperies, for a kitchen with linoleum flooring and a bright overhead light that signaled serious tasting, not a social occasion.

Rowan arrived and said, for about the hundredth time since I'd requested his help, "I'm not exactly sure what you want me to do."

"Taste the wine!" I said, "For God's sake, you've done that before."

He glanced at the paper bag. I wondered, briefly, if he'd been hiding a gourmet snobbery from me, the sort of finely tuned tastes that can't handle lowbrow wine. He had the wiry frame of a picky eater and wrote articles for gourmet-minded readers. I considered the evidence.

"Well," Rowan said before I could accuse him, "what are we looking at?"

He removed the bottles and lined them up for inspection. I collected two fistfuls of wine glasses and explained the rationale behind my purchases. He scrunched one eyebrow up in an exaggerated expression of doubt. I offered him some whiskey to start. He accepted. Then, we opened the Bordeaux.

"Candied violets?" Rowan asked when he read the description. "This guy has never eaten a candied violet in his life."

He poured a little into a glass. A few drops landed on the pocket of his white shirt, a vibrant purple. So far the description held true.

"Violets?" I prompted.

"They're not leaping out at me."

With the violets dismissed, we got down to business exploring the full array of wines. We poured. We breathed in the aromas. We took some exploratory sips.

"You have to chew it," Rowan said. I gave him the same look Eric got with the coffee spoon slurping. "I'm serious. Like food."

Technically, you're aerating the wine, upping that retronasal olfaction, and making sure the wine touches all the taste receptors in your mouth. Rowan has mastered the wine chewing, sort of rolling silent *R*s through it, while pacing and looking pensive. The best I could do was swishing it like mouthwash.

Nothing tasted strongly of raisin or black cherry or green apple. The Bordeaux tasted jammy. We focused on Gregory's wine.

"Strawberry," Rowan said.

I sniffed and swished and sipped. I tried it twice, then on the third time, like magic—strawberry.

"Okay," I said, "I get strawberry. Give me something else."

Rowan chewed his wine and thought for a while. When he finished thinking he had a list: "Strawberry, more flowery, perfume-y, less jammy [than the Bordeaux], more acidity or tangy ... cocoa ... although I get my cocoa and tobacco confused."

I swished some more. "I can taste tobacco now, but I'm pretty sure that's just because I'm impressionable."

Rowan picked up a Merlot. He took a sip. "Sawdust," he announced, "sort of like the inside of your grandmother's cabinets. Or maybe that's just my grandmother."

Yes, I could catch that after a few tries, too.

It would be fair to ask whether my perception of the strawberry, tobacco, and sawdust had much validity since I seemed to head in whatever direction Rowan pointed. He could be basing those directions on nothing. Less cynically, perhaps I tasted those notes because he was correct and a physical stimulation that said "tobacco" really did linger in the Pinot. At the very least I was experiencing new dimensions in wine flavor. I'd moved beyond the threshold of an overpowering "sour grape juice" signal, and now I tried to turn off my logical memorization of flavor elements and allow my senses to retrieve them instinctively. It felt awkward, but it was an improvement.

Lawrence arrived home and poured himself a glass of wine from the table. Finally Rowan had someone who could match him in flavor knowledge. Plenty of Lawrence's master brewer skills translated into the wine world. He settled into a kitchen chair, and the two men were ready to reminisce about the wines of their past.

"Tell us about the port," I prompted Lawrence. I may not know wine tasting, but I know which of his collection of wine tasting stories other wine people enjoy.

"I remember this time, in the Hotel Boulderado," he said. "I was on the board of the Brewers Association of America and I was the youngest board member by far. We were at a meeting and wound up downstairs in this antique bar, and somebody bought a bottle of port ..." The story went on that he had never tasted port as anything but a side attraction to a cheese plate before. Now, with brewers who both understood port and spoke the same flavor language he did, he paid attention. The ports revealed myriad dried fruit notes, some with spiciness; some were earthy, some smoky, some hot (meaning the alcohol came through more strongly).

"But the thing is, we were tasting in the wrong order," Lawrence said. "From the least expensive to the most expensive." Lawrence sat at the "most expensive" end of the line.

The next person bought a bottle and sent the bottle around. Then the next person. The final port on the list, the one that would land on Lawrence's tab, would cost him as much as the entire trip to Boulder. It was "long past the evening and moving towards morning" when, one order away from Lawrence's turn, the waitress announced last call and cut them off.

"And what did you learn about port flavor from drinking those expensive bottles?" I asked.

"That it got better."

The men started a second round of wine sampling, tsk-tsking about the purple color, the jammy-ness, the American attitude towards wine that wanted it to taste like juice.

In his twenties, Lawrence used to travel to Fiesole, to his friend's grandmother's farm, to help with the grape harvest. He'd fly in a few

34

days early and travel from winery to winery across Tuscany. When he found a wine he connected with in that moment, he'd buy enough to last the rest of the trip, to drink with the rabbits they shot in the fields and smoked with grape vines in a wood fired oven. The wine came in bottles protected by woven baskets large enough to carry several days' worth of laundry.

Rowan remembered putting all his college spending money towards wine. Wine bottles circled his dorm room.

"We drank Canadian Club," I said. "Where were you at school? Napa Valley?"

Florida, as it turns out. I'd had a Floridian wine. It tasted like mixing equal parts orange juice and coffee.

"I was reading a lot of Hemingway," Rowan remembered. He loved the idea that there were areas in France that were the only place you could go to taste a particular wine. That thought led Lawrence straight back to Italy, and then they moved on to places they'd like to go to drink unusual wine. The list included Moldova.

Later that evening, sitting down to a late dinner, Lawrence brought out a glass of wine from the kitchen for the two of us to share. And I *knew* which one it was (Gregory's Pinot Noir).

"That's pretty good for me," I said.

"Mmm," he said.

"That bottle of wine you have marked 'Do Not Open'—why is it for a special occasion?"

Because, as it turned out, his friends had given it to him.

"We can open that wine whenever you want," Lawrence said.

"But it's for a special occasion."

He shrugged.

"I need to practice more."

He agreed to that, too.

However, I did not feel as if I needed to practice any more that particular night. I liberated the bottle of whiskey I'd first offered Rowan from where we kept it hidden on the cellar stairs. This particular liquor, Rail Dog, was a new kind of distilled spirit, one that used maple syrup as a base and aged in oak barrels for eighteen months. Its label proclaimed, "Now Maple Has Its Spirit."

Maple's spirit tasted somewhere between delicate rum and cognac. It was not very sweet, and what sweetness existed had a complexity reflecting the maple syrup from which it's distilled. The scent brought me back to reading when I was a child. In elementary school, when I got a new paperback book, the paper would be slightly rough and the paper smell would be so intoxicating that I'd press my tongue to the pages. Then I'd throw myself into the world of the book, transfixed, for hours at a time. The maple spirit returned that childhood emotion of standing on the precipice of stories, heady with the scent of the books that held them. If breakfast cereal could be my reminder that I have the capacity for tasting subtle flavor differences, then spirits would be my reminder that flavors can also spark emotions and memories. I could imagine wine in the same role one day.

CHAPTER FOUR

FLAVOR COMBINATIONS

WINE TASTINGS EXERCISE OUR ABILITY to pay close attention to a complex flavor. These tastings also miss a key component of wine for most people—we drink it with food. Comparative tastings exist for the benefit of people interested in studying a flavor, not as part of our normal course of life. In real life, a bottle of Chianti should by all rights appear alongside a plate of pasta. When I tasted the Stellenbosch Shiraz at the wine trade show, I didn't just think of South Africa, I thought of South African *braais*. As wine merchant Kevin Lynch puts it, "When a woman chooses a hat, she does not put it on a goat's head; she puts it on her own. There is a vast difference, an insurmountable difference, between the taste of a wine next to another wine, and the same wine's taste with food[22]."

You can invest as much, perhaps more, effort in combining wine with food as in understanding the wine in the first place. Lynch goes on to explain that a wine paired with the right food can "stand up and dance like Baryshnikov," and decades of study can go into finding those pairings that will dance. Still, don't let the wine connoisseurs' search for the knockout, soul mate, perfect food and wine couplings mislead you; the rest of us also engage in flavor pairing work every day. It's not as flashy as Baryshnikov, but it may be the single most common act of food creativity: putting something together for dinner (or lunch, or breakfast, or a snack). You might even say we evolved to do this work, piecing together different foods to give us all the nutrition we needed back in the hunter-gatherer days. As individuals in the modern age, we reach for the ketchup to dip our fries in or coffee to dunk our doughnuts or beer to go with our pizza without even thinking about it.

---

22 *Adventures on the Wine Route* (1988) 13.

We are instinctive combiners of flavor—wine with our food, foods on a menu, ingredients that make a dish. Our eating lives revolve around flavor combinations. The question, then, is, *What makes them work?*

Researchers have no consensus on what makes flavors go together. Theories float around rooted in data sets or a chef's artistry or random chance. In 2011, a team of researchers from Northeastern University and Harvard University published a paper testing a theory espoused by some chefs that flavors pair well together when they share a certain number of chemical compounds.[23] One example from the paper is white chocolate and caviar (which share trimethylamine and other flavor compounds). After cataloguing thousands of recipes and the chemical compounds behind them, the team found that American cuisine groups like flavors, as the chefs claimed. But in Asian cuisine the opposite is true, pairing *unlike* flavors. Another study, this one from the Monell Institute, suggests that mouthfeel accounts for the strongest pairings, so that, for example, fatty foods go with acidic foods—like dry red wine with lamb, or an IPA with ribs.[24] Still other researchers find that food pairings mostly exist in our own minds. If we're *told* a wine and a food go together, we'll taste pairing characteristics that we wouldn't otherwise detect.[25] Other respected researchers offer other theories. Basically, the question remains wide open.

I'm moving my own inquiry forward. It's based on the observation that bacon pairs with almost everything. Some people might go so far as to say that everything is *better* with bacon. Even wine.

I know that wine and bacon pair together because every Thursday is Chocolate, Bacon, and Wine Night at a local bar and chocolate shop called Nutty Steph's. The proprietress at Nutty Steph's is a vegetarian who recently changed her name from Stephanie to Jacqueline and decorated her establishment as if you're backstage at a burlesque show

23 You can find it at http://www.nature.com in the December 2011 issue, "Flavor Network and the Principles of Food Pairing."

24 From a *Scientific American* podcast posted 10/15/12 at http://www.scientificamerican .com/podcast/episode/food-pairings-rely-on-mouthfeel-12-10-15

25 Wells, Peter. Does Wine Taste Better with Food? *Food and Wine* April 2006 (accessed at http://www.foodandwine.com 2/13/14). This article profiles the work of Dr. Hildegarde Heymann at UC-Davis.

in an unspecified European country—lots of red and black and flap-per-ish fringes on the edges of objects. The customers on Thursday nights wear ironic mustaches. Jacqueline is deeply invested in the Nutty part of her brand, which began with a granola that contained generous amounts of almonds, walnuts, and hazelnuts and has since diversified.

Nutty Steph's weekly plates of bacon, chocolate, and wine work as more than a marketing gimmick. Say what you want about bacon crazes—these items *do* pair together. For one thing, when we're talking about bacon, we're talking about salt *and* fat *and* an aroma that is, frankly, salacious; bacon short-circuits all thought and focuses my senses only on desire. If vegetarians employ a celebrity exemption rule to their plates, that celebrity is bacon. Food researchers, manufactur-ers, and chefs have demonstrated that pumping up a food's aroma, salt, fat, and also sugar far beyond the home cook's comfort zone affects (positively) the pleasure we get from it. Bacon brings the aroma/salt/fat intensity all on its own.

The combination of bacon, wine, and chocolate flavors creates a balanced plate. Think of the first taste to hit you in each of these foods. Bacon is salty and savory. Chocolate is sweet and bitter. Red wine is tart. Together, we have all five tastes. Think about the texture. Bacon is crispy and fatty at the same time—you get both the crunch and the sucking of grease off fingertips. Chocolate is something solid to bite into, then soft on your tongue, and it adds to the fatty mouthfeel. Wine is astringent and cuts through the fat. The feel of these ingredients cre-ates balance, too.

On an even closer examination, wine, chocolate, and bacon are all foods that can deliver complex flavors, and their subtler notes can match each other. The smokiness and spiciness in the bacon can find its echo in the aromas and flavors of a red wine. Some red Zinfandels, for example, are smoky and peppery, and the aroma of bacon itself can appear in a Syrah. Chocolate can have a smoky or spicy quality, while its sweetness might match up with the caramelization on the edge of fried bacon strips. You can also think of how these subtler fla-vors reflect more traditional bacon complements. At breakfast you'd eat bacon with your coffee, which has a bitter taste, as does chocolate, and coffee can also have acidic berry notes, like what you might find in red wine. Buttermilk pancakes are slightly sour and also slightly sweet, like wine is both sour and sweet. Maple syrup (the real kind) has a complex, earthy sweetness, something that chocolates can echo. Bacon fits in well. All three elements—bacon, chocolate, and wine—both complement and contrast each other. They do not clash.

The other senses simply reinforce a happy culinary occasion. All these items smell great, sound great (bacon sizzling, cork popping from a wine bottle), and the bawdy visual cues of Nutty Steph's bar point towards decadence. Perfect.

We can look back on bacon's success and point to reasons that might explain popular flavor pairings like cupcakes with bacon brittle frosting, bacon kettle corn, and bacon-wrapped dates/shrimp/scallops/olives/whole turkeys. With this hindsight, we're building a framework for predicting a winning flavor combination—like thinking if bacon goes well with maple syrup, it probably goes well with other sweet and complex things, which means it would go well with a high-end bitter-sweet chocolate bar. In this instance it would be a conscious exercise, but we also have dozens (or more) frameworks our minds refer to every day without us even realizing it, built through our experience of eating dishes that *other* people have already discovered work.

Think about a sandwich. What is a sandwich if not a decision about a variation of protein (deli meat, hamburger, tuna, peanut butter) with tangy and sweet condiments (mayonnaise, ketchup, mustard, jelly) between two slices of bread? If we did not have a "sandwich" framework we could not have the "build your own" section of the deli board. Think of the common dinner combination of spaghetti, marinara sauce, and a green salad. Like the bacon plate, this balances both textures and flavors, and we can think about how to swap equivalents in and out to make new, pleasing combinations. You could rewrite that dinner menu as a framework with potential variations: a neutral starch (spaghetti, gnocchi, macaroni, pizza dough) with something tangy (tomatoes, sharp cheese, olives) and a crunchy vegetable side (green salad, crudité, cucumber slices). Spices can work the same way. I gather together lime juice, sugar, fish sauce, and chiles (a Vietnamese framework) and I can apply it to noodles, ground pork, tofu, fish or any of a half-dozen bases, and it will taste good. Or something that goes with sweet, like cinnamon, cloves, and ginger, a combination that could go into pies, crisps, cookies, chutneys, and jams.

We could loosely summarize all of world cuisine as a long series of trial and error to build basic frameworks that predict good flavor combinations. Avid cooks may have a larger store of these equations committed to memory, and we may have varying degrees of bravery in how far afield we'll go when swapping new ingredients into the mix, but anyone who has ever navigated a salad bar knows the essential process. The next question is how these tried and true methods for coming up with a pleasing dish might be extended to more inventive cuisine. After all, the universe of known flavor combinations that work (i.e. taste like something that you'd like another bite of) isn't static. Everyone from adventurous home cooks to award-winning chefs pushes at the edges of what has been tried before.

A few blocks from my house, a small restaurant constantly finds new ways to assemble flavors. They have to because their menus change completely every three weeks. Suzanne Podhaizer opened Salt Café after four years as a food critic for Vermont's weekly paper, *Seven Days*. Hers is a small restaurant (only twenty seats) that caters to people interested in knowing all the details of their meal, details like the weather conditions under which their strawberries were harvested or the feed on which the entrée's ducks were raised. I'm sure Suzanne would never say her most loyal customers are insufferable foodies, but I'll say it. It's a clientele that won't be satisfied with any old menu. The former food critic has to answer to a customer base of amateur food critics with menus that show creativity and skill.

The dining room design encourages customers to ponder how Salt might invent its dishes and assemble its menus. One corner houses an enviable cookbook collection, available for customers to browse through should their dinner dates prove less interesting than, say, the dishes of *Seduced by Bacon*. Suzanne's cookbooks let customers daydream about being a restaurant proprietor, wandering into work on a sunny morning, sitting with a mug of tea and leafing through the collection to gather inspiration for the next gourmet meal. Suzanne is upfront about the fact that her life doesn't really work that way, that it's hectic, full of anxiety about deliveries that don't show up on time, about making payroll, paying bills, meeting city codes, and (somewhere on that list) worrying about the next menu. I enjoy the cookbook daydream anyway. When I stopped by to ask Suzanne about how she comes up with her dishes, she was, in fact, sitting amidst the cookbooks, holding a mug of tea, although she was busy fretting about goose supply shortages, not browsing.

I started out with quizzing Suzanne on her attitudes towards bacon as a universal ingredient. She is pro-bacon, and, she added, she stands firm on bacon as part of dessert, even if some people consider it too trendy. "Bacon hits all the right buttons in our brain," she said. "There's salt, smoke, fat, sweet ... Bacon-caramel is a good pairing, maple pudding with bacon brittle, candied bacon on chocolate flourless cake."

I've never had any of those three desserts at Salt, but I made a note to watch for them.

We chatted about highlights that stayed in my mind from past Salt menus. My favorite dishes, it turned out, don't actually pair two flavors at all. Instead, they double down on a single flavor. Like their version of Jell-O. Here, squeezing the juice from a Meyer lemon, tangerine, or blood orange gives you the essential flavor of the fruit. Simmering that juice reduces it and concentrates the flavor. Gelatin then returns that flavorful juice to a solid structure. It's intensified the fruit without adding any outside flavor. At Salt I once sipped a broth that tasted like an entire duck in the bowl of my spoon. For another dish, Suzanne roasted wild mushrooms then poured on truffle oil for a serious woodland mushroom taste, which proved inspired.

Strong single flavors don't appear as often in cooking as combined flavors do, and I have to admit that those intense-flavor dishes aren't the ones I usually order. I'd stumbled on them through the kindness of a former Salt chef who, realizing I passed over the best items, would send out samples of what I'd missed. When fending for myself, I can't help believing that I'm getting my money's worth only when I see a long list of ingredients. This attitude implies that enjoying a dinner is like tallying profits on an accounting sheet—the more you add together the better it is. I know it doesn't work that way ... Still, "escabeche: pickled baby turnips, fiddleheads, radishes, ramps and egg, Parmesan-cracked pepper dip" sounds better as an appetizer than "duck broth," even though I have no idea what *escabeche* means and I love the duck broth.

My attitude towards the simple, single-flavor dishes is part of a larger challenge Suzanne faces. Her customers arrive with all sorts of preconceptions about what the menu should look like, and they don't always agree. Some people want to see long lists of ingredients, most want to see uber-local ingredients, some want something creative that others would categorize as weird and off-putting. All want something they wouldn't make at home but something that will leave them as satisfied as a comfortable, home-cooked meal. I asked Suzanne about her "tried and true" flavor combinations, the ones no customer would ever question.

"Hmmm," she paused briefly, then listed beets and goat cheese, walnuts and blue cheese, potatoes and poultry fat.

Really? Of all the potato options, poultry fat sprang to mind first?

I tried again with what her favorite unusual flavor pairings would be, ones that work but aren't obvious. "Salt and bananas, applesauce with shallots in it, cheese with chocolate … like goat cheese on a flourless chocolate cake." She later admitted that, to her, goat cheese goes with everything. I would posit that flourless chocolate cake also goes with everything. A flourless chocolate cake made with goat cheese and a praline bacon sprinkle on top would be delicious.

Suzanne also looks for pairings that bring out flavors otherwise too subtle to notice, like adding butter and almonds to rice to highlight the grain's nuttiness. Similarly, she would make a warm grain salad with blood orange, olive oil, and parsley because "I'm not going to just eat a pile of spelt and wheat berries."

I wouldn't eat a pile of spelt berries, either, but for different reasons… like the fact that spelt berries don't hang out in my cupboards.

To be fair, even though I don't currently dish up bowls of spelt in my kitchen, I can see how I'd get to thinking about the best spelt combinations if I were a chef. If I had lots of time in a kitchen and the pressure to come up with restaurant menus, I'd choose a mildly unusual ingredient like spelt and then play around with it. Maybe someone with a more refined palate could taste a forkful and think it had a delicate nutty yet vegetal taste crying out for flavorful olive oil and blood orange. But it also wouldn't be cheating to start by cooking up a big batch and then dumping random sauces on each successive bite until something clicked. Or, I could start by looking up the results from *someone else* doing that—in other words, checking a cookbook or two and then improvising from there. Suzanne did use the cookbooks in her corner for menu building when she began the restaurant. She would spread six or seven out in front of her on the table and open to the relevant dish or cuisine she wanted on that menu rotation, then take the pieces she liked most from each writer's approach to create her own versions. Known successful combinations led the way to something new.

Cookbook immersion, along with spending a lot of time with a single ingredient or flavor, helps when learning about food. Both strategies eventually became too inefficient in making the three-week menu cycles Salt relies on. Suzanne says that today, most of the work of coming up with menus happens in her imagination. The "brain mouth," one of her chefs called it. In the same way that people learning a foreign language eventually reach the point of putting together a conversation without rushing to a dictionary, people learning about food eventually can put together a dish without outside reference. Just as someone might learn to think in French or Spanish, Suzanne has learned to think in flavors.

For those of us who have not learned to think in flavors, we're fortunate that many chefs will share their knowledge. In 2008, *The Flavor Bible* asked top chefs around the world for their recommended flavor pairings or affinities. Their compiled answers became a reference book for looking up an ingredient and finding a list of other ingredients that chefs use with it, a sort of culinary rhyming dictionary. This guidance allows amateurs like me to piece together recipes using the sort of flavor matches that come to chefs as second nature. It feels much cooler than using a recipe.

I put *The Flavor Bible*'s invitation to creativity to the test soon after I acquired it by building a 26-"course" dinner from its pages.[26] The courses were really ingredients, each in its own bowl, placed in a circle around the edge of our dining room table. I started with mozzarella, chose one of its flavor affinities—anchovies (I happen to like anchovies)—looked at the entry for *that* ingredient and chose tomatoes with balsamic vinegar, and so on back to mozzarella again. My menu for the evening read like this:

> Mozzarella → Anchovies → Tomatoes with Balsamic Vinegar → Almonds → Prunes → Orange → Arugula → Bacon → Lentils → Coconut → Pistachios → Rice → Potatoes → Celery → Capers → Onions (cooked) → Apples → Mustard → Cucumbers → Buttermilk → Dates → Bananas → Sesame → Shrimp → Beer → Cured Meat → Mozzarella. Plus bread and butter.

Unsure whether it was a brilliant dinner plan or something that would feel like grazing a salad bar one boring bite at a time, I limited the guest list to my friends Nick and Claire. Nick is Canadian, and just as I can make endless variations on a sandwich, he and Claire can make unlimited variations on poutine. The traditional Canadian dish of fries, cheese curds, and gravy appears in many forms when the two of them have a hand in dinner, including as Thanksgiving poutine (with cranberry relish and stuffing beneath the gravy), Chinese buffet poutine (with a hoisin sauce-gravy hybrid), and cocktail party poutine (a tater tot and cheese curd on a toothpick with gravy dip). Claire does not hesitate to experiment at her own dinner parties. Shortly before I invited her over for the 26-dish dinner, she threw a party to finish off 13 pounds of pork that she needed out of her freezer. The dinner culminated in a cake made with shredded pork, apple, and cheddar, with maple cream cheese frosting. The cake was undeniably sweet, but the pork, instead of clashing with the dessert sweetness, added depth to the flavor so that the character of all the ingredients—including the

---

26 Why 26? Because at the time I was reading Peter Sagal's "Gluttony" chapter in *The Book of Vice* (It Books, 2008) where he dines on 26 courses at Alinea, a Chicago restaurant.

apple, cheese, and maple—didn't disappear in a sugary rush. Claire claimed never to have doubted it would taste great.

My own 26-course experiment worked out better than I'd predicted. We circled the table in order first. I learned that buttermilk tastes surprisingly good sipped alone and even better with dates. I reaffirmed the near-perfection of beer alongside cured meats. I learned that celery is not a neutral crunchy vegetable stick that exists to eat with Buffalo chicken wings but in fact has its own character, marrying the refreshing lightness of cucumber with an herbal flavor that hints at old fashioned lovage or angelica, which are in the same plant family. It pairs well with capers. When we'd gone around once, we had flavor combination ideas already seeded for going back again. Tomatoes and anchovies on thickly buttered bread. Shrimp and mozzarella wrapped in a slice of salami. Apples, potatoes, onions, and mustard. Celery, capers, and potatoes. Lentils, bacon, arugula, and orange … everything we tried worked. It seemed so easy to invent new dishes! Then again, of course it seemed easy—I was using the collected wisdom of people who've spent their whole careers developing an instinct for what flavors go together.

Combining flavors into something that satisfies your particular palate takes trial and error, but it's trial and error with plenty of shortcuts. You can start with a universally appealing ingredient like bacon that enhances many, many dishes and simply add it in and see what happens. You can pay attention to the frameworks you already know, like pizza crust + sauce + toppings, and try new combinations within those. You can find cookbooks that don't just provide recipes but also provide guidance for branching out with variations on the base recipe. You can choose an ingredient, like spelt, and play around with it and see what happens. And when you need more inspiration, it may be time to browse the menus of creative restaurants where skilled chefs have spent more hours than I want to contemplate seeking out flavor combinations that work.

Of course, the problem with trial and error is that you have to both be willing to accept experiments that don't work and keep an open mind about what will work. Maintaining that open mind can be tricky.

I'll look at recipes from my mother's childhood and wrinkle my nose at suggestions like tuna Jell-O pie, bananas hollandaise, and ribbon cake with ham, eggs, and cream cheese[27]—but I enjoyed Claire's pork cake and accepted Suzanne's suggestion of salt with bananas, which aren't that far off from the vintage recipe list. Besides, an entire generation enjoyed the Jell-O-anything, processed meat-craving, liver-accepting cookbook concoctions of the 1950s, so who am I to judge?

---

27 These particular examples are from "21 Truly Upsetting Vintage Recipes" at http://www.buzzfeed.com, accessed 1/11/14.

CHAPTER FIVE

THE ARTISAN MYSTIQUE

For SEVERAL YEARS I kept an empty box of Artisan Vermont White Cheddar Cheese Wheat Thins on a shelf in my kitchen. I worked at Vermont's Agency of Agriculture Food and Markets at the time and imagined that one day I'd find a reason to use this box as a prop in a speech—should state government ever see fit to allow me to make speeches (which they didn't). In the meantime, it sat waiting for some visitor to inquire and for me to declare:

"There are no artisan Vermont cheese Wheat Thins!"

Which would be true both because the box was empty and because there is no such thing as artisan Wheat Thins, only plain old mass-produced Wheat Thins that come in different flavors. These particular Wheat Thins were coated in a cheese powder from a Vermont company, just as Wheat Thins Ranch are coated in a ranch dressing powder from some other company somewhere else. I happen to find the Vermont cheese powder version to be the most irresistible variety of Wheat Thins ever, but irresistible and artisan are not the same thing.

The dictionary defines "artisan" or "artisanal" as something produced in small quantities by skilled craftspeople. In marketing, it's a term of art applied to foods neither produced in small quantities nor as the handiwork of a skilled craftsperson. However, the artisan concept points to some important distinctions in how our food tastes. It moves us out from evaluating a single dish to look at food *system* factors, such as how our food is researched, developed, processed, and transported. These factors shape the flavors on our plate. In broad terms we can think of artisan (the dictionary definition kind) as one of three types of foods, a third way between homemade and mass-produced.

Let's start on one end of the food production spectrum with home-made. Homemade food comes from a kitchen and is made from basic ingredients.. Apples. Eggs. Flour. Generally speaking, the ingredients that go into a homemade item do not, themselves, have ingredients. A brownie mix, on the other hand, might produce brownies baked at home but doesn't count as "homemade." When I create something truly homemade in my kitchen, I get to make it to my personal spec-ifications. I'm in control of selecting the ingredients, deciding which recipe I want to use, and modifying any recipe on any whim at any time during the cooking process. Everyone has a different style of home cooking. Because of this individuality within homemade food, we end up with phrases like an apple pie that "tastes just like my mother made." Homemade items carry the imprimatur of the cook, for better or for worse.

Let's look at the pie example. My mother raised me to be picky about pie crust. Her crust uses a simple recipe of shortening, flour, and water. After many years of internal conflict, I've migrated away from my mother's pie crust recipe. In fact, I've adopted a whole portfolio of pie crust recipes, because in my own kitchen I'm entitled to bake as I please. For strawberry- rhubarb pies and lemon pies, I use a butter and cream crust that is both flaky and soft and has a delicate dairy taste. I have a sturdier butter and flour recipe for pumpkin pie, chess pies, and the occasional banana cream pie. For berry pies, I use butter, shortening, and a little sugar in the crust to bring sweetness all the way through the pastry. I still use my mother's shortening crust recipe for chicken pot pies and peach pie because I like the weight of the crust and how the neutral shortening doesn't compete at all with the flavors of savory gravy or thick peach syrup. Other pie crust bakers go further. Melissa Clark wrote for the *New York Times* about her own search for the best fat to use in a pie crust,[28] which covered the additional terri-tory of olive oil, canola oil, grape seed oil, coconut oil, ghee, nut but-ters, then a suite of animal fats—beef suet, duck fat, regular lard, and leaf lard (from the fat that surrounds a hog's kidneys). She stopped short of goose fat, marrow, foie gras, browned butter, truffle butter, or

---

28 "Heaven in a Pie Plate" (2006)

bear fat. You won't replace this sort of comparative crust baking with comparative pre-made crust shopping.

The companies mass-producing pie crusts (enough to satisfy national demand … or at least everyone on their side of the Mississippi) face practical limitations in what they can put on the shelves. Those limitations do not allow for duck fat. If you're one of these companies, you need a final recipe that meets the cost ceiling for ingredients, has a long shelf life, can be transported easily around the country, can be produced in high volume (which usually means by machines), and looks pleasing to potential customers (my pies rarely look pleasing). Some latitude exists within these variables. For example, you won't always use the cheapest ingredient if a slightly more expensive one will significantly improve sales. Even so, the pre-made foods I buy in the supermarket, unlike the homemade ones I place on my table, have not arrived through recipes based on a whim.

For a long time, companies approached problems like deciding on a crust recipe by looking at their constraints and finding a recipe within those parameters that they deemed to be better than their competitors'. The logic resembles dreaded high school math problem sets for calculating "optimal" solutions across multiple equations—like if you have a triangle inside a sphere rolling over a parabola, what's the highest point the tip of the triangle can reach? Except, while we can trust that the person writing the high school math book had a correct answer, the real world gets messier. The optimal pie doesn't exist, not really, because people have different tastes. So the question becomes not only who can get closest to that highest point on the tip of the triangle on the parabola, but also whether that point is something worth searching for in the first place.

Anyone who has gathered a large group of friends and family for Thanksgiving dinner has navigated the issue of optimizing for different tastes. Dark meat versus white meat versus vegetarian turkey alternatives, smooth cranberry relish versus chunky, white potatoes versus sweet potatoes, baked versus mashed, the controversial marshmallows on a casserole dish. For decades my family has had at least three cranberry relish options, and for twenty years I've brought the soft pretzel rolls I'd learned to make in seventh grade home economics class because these please everybody. Families everywhere negotiate these Thanksgiving dinner type situations, but how would someone scale the solutions up for products that appeal to millions of customers? Is the answer to have as many different cranberry relishes as it takes for everyone to find what they want? And how many would that be? Three? Dozens? Hundreds? Or should you do your best to find the equivalent of seventh grade soft pretzels, the universal crowd pleasers?

For many years, food companies went for the soft pretzel solution—one option that hit a perfect compromise between everybody's tastes—and stuck to it. A generation ago, the thinking began to change. Those "perfect" recipes were proving too imperfect, and competitors could step in to scoop up customers left less than fully satisfied. Plus, technology had changed, making it easier to offer multiple variations on a core product. Researchers looked at their data again. Instead of calculating the single best option within the various business constraints (cost, shelf life, consistency, and so on), they tried to understand what the results of consumer testing told them if they took away the "one answer" constraint. They discovered that customers grouped around distinct preferences, not infinite ones. For example, if the results of taste testing showed customers split into two salsa preference profiles, one group that liked mild-chunky salsa and one that liked spicy-smooth salsa, you would make those two options and not bother with mild-smooth or spicy-chunky. If salsa fans fell into many more camps, then you could narrow them down with additional considerations, such as the relative popularity of each, or which distinguished you most from the competition, or which offered the highest profit margin. The important lesson was identifying clusters of preference that cut through all the possible variations on a food, and then finding the defining differences—the ones that would determine which group someone belonged to.

Harold Moskowitz pioneered many of the strategies transitioning towards this product diversity. His 2007 book *Selling Blue Elephants* describes his experimental design. Companies first list the key elements of their product that they could vary, many of which will sound familiar from the basic flavor vocabulary: the amount of bitter or sour or sweet, the appearance, mouthfeel, aroma, and so on. Researchers then create prototypes. Consumer tasting panels sample each proto-type then respond to questions about it, testing their preference for every element on the list. Statisticians look at the results and start to delineate groups based on clusters of preferences. Not every element is going to be a strong differentiator between groups, so food compa-nies can focus on the ones that fit together into a particular customer profile. In coffee, for example, Moskowitz found that while nearly everyone asked for a "rich, robust flavor"—the potentially perfect single coffee everyone had been searching for—in reality we fall into three preference camps: strong and bitter, rich aroma and moderate strength, weak coffee. Tasters also fell into three levels for the amount of bitterness they liked. A coffee business could then offer three dif-ferent products that matched the observed preferences and leave it to the marketers to figure out how to pitch them to a nation of individu-als who erroneously believe their own perfect cup of coffee has a rich, robust flavor.

Diversity begets diversity, and once one coffee company offers three choices, another will come up with four, then five. Moskowitz worked with Prego to introduce regular tomato sauce, spicy sauce, and the never-before-seen chunky sauce. Ragú responded with its own varieties. Fifteen years of escalation later, Ragú now has 36 varieties of pasta sauce. The ultimate result is that today we expect to see multiple variations on every company's product. Food companies reinforce our sense of endless choices by making changes that don't change flavor at all but instead repackage the product to catch customers' eyes, like all those Christmas colored candies that get end-of-aisle displays in season.

Even with recent changes, a grocery aisle still can't come close to providing the choices available to a home cook. The equation may have shifted to include multiple answers, but those limiting factors remain relevant. Leaf lard simply is not available in quantities to sat-isfy a product line at Pillsbury. And there's the expense. At a national volume of production, even a fraction of a penny price difference adds up to serious budget considerations. At home, I might not spring for leaf lard, but I wouldn't switch ingredients to save a mere penny on my one crust. Large companies also don't want recipes like my super-delicate butter and cream crust that would end up as nothing but crumbs if it were boxed and shipped after baking. Employees on a production floor don't move by cravings—dusting maple sugar across the top crust of a pear pie without warning or cutting butter into the shortening. Each pie is uniform. Perhaps most harsh of all, in the commercial food world, if a flavor doesn't have high enough sales to justify its existence, it's removed from the line regardless of how much you or I might personally love it (I'm talking to you, Ben & Jerry, for discontinuing Rainforest Crunch Ice Cream.)[29]

Home cooks face their own constraints. Homemade variations are theoretically endless but practically limited by factors like a cook's patience for rendering lard or whether her curiosity extends to bear fat (even as I write this, I'm wondering where I could source some). There are also skill constraints. I bought a cookbook of how to make magazine-shoot-worthy pastries. My version of the "easy" cake ended with batter dyed pink and green and entirely raw in the middle; I picked out the fully baked chunks, mushed them up with chocolate frosting, smashed it into a cake pan, spread another layer of frosting on top, and called it a day. And then we have the issue of special equipment and supplies; my home ice cream maker does not perform like a commercial version, and Lawrence refuses to home brew beer after enjoying the precision of professional brewing equipment. And who is going to eat my 100 pie experiments? Or clean up after inventing 37 pasta sauces? Everyone has limits.

In between the limitations of homemade and the limitations of mass-produced, we find the artisan food maker. Artisan implies something akin to another home cook taking the trouble to bake a pie and then sell it to you. Except, this home cook has advantages that an actual home cook does not have. An artisan producer focuses on one productor a few;; they're not taking on responsibility for feeding a household or even making a complete meal. This focus gives the producer a chance to practice skills and develop recipes that taste exactly the way they want. Small-scale producers can invest in equipment that

---

29 The Ben & Jerry's Vermont office even have a flavor graveyard.

makes sense for a business but not for the average kitchen collection. This equipment can make a big difference in quality and consistency. Artisan cheese makers have caves for aging cheese in, instead of drafty basement corners; craft beer brewers use temperature-controlled steam kettles for producing the wort. Artisan producers can also deal directly with specialty ingredient suppliers to make sure that, for example, they have a reliable supply of rendered leaf lard—I would have to hope for a lucky find when I visited a butcher.

Artisan food producers, as a business, also have some advantages national brands do not have. They share an implicit understanding with their customers that they may charge higher prices in return for prioritizing quality ingredients and flavor over margin.[30] Because their operations (and their competitors' operations) are small-scale and not fully mechanized, they can consider recipes that require a human touch. Because their business model relies on a much smaller customer base, they have the option of covering a smaller market area, reducing transportability challenges. Small-scale producers have business constraints, too. They still need to think about costs—customers are price flexible to a point, then they get anxious. They still need products to be able to ship farther than the trip from the kitchen to the dining table. They need to worry about shelf life. They need the right packaging. They need to please more people's tastes than simply their own and immediate family members', but they don't have a Harold Moskowitz on staff to figure out how. They need recipes that will scale up from serving a family to serving hundreds, then thousands, of people while still tasting like something prepared for only a few. It's not quite as simple as baking an extra pie and selling it to your neighbor.

My friend Claire, the same woman behind the pork cake, understands the realities of being a very small-scale food producer. She owns Butterfly Bakery, which sells cookies, granola, and scones wholesale,

---

30 "Quality ingredient" sounds judgmental here, but it's also true that some ingredients are premium ingredients, priced out of the range of many conventional food producers. We're about to get into that more with maple syrup as a sweetener. Wonderful to have, expensive to acquire.

plus an array of other treats (including hot sauce) at the local Farmers' Market. She does not currently offer pork-based baked goods. Butterfly Bakery qualifies as artisan by anyone's standards. It's just Claire, in a kitchen that passed a commercial inspection. Visit Claire's kitchen and you'll find her mixing ingredients in wide metal bowls that she spins like a pottery wheel or scooping cookie dough into perfectly measured rounds in rows on large baking sheets. Both activities are mesmerizing. The whole operation smells great, perfuming the bakery's occupants with cinnamon, vanilla, and maple syrup for the rest of the day.

When I asked Claire to tell me about her recipe development process, she suggested that I remind everyone not to say that her cookies are good "for a vegan cookie."

"What is it about vegan cookies?" Claire asked. "I'm not even vegan. I'm making a tasty cookie. One of the first food reporters to write about my cookies liked them, but then she said they were 'good for being vegan.' Awesome. Thanks."

Claire never, ever uses the word "awesome" to describe something positive.

I first met Claire over a large chocolate chip-peanut butter cookie. I was sitting outside a downtown café. She lived in the apartment above the café and was trucking boxes of cookies down the stairs to her minivan. Claire can lug a *lot* of boxes at once. She stands almost six feet tall and, at that time, she fit a lot of weight onto that frame. She gained minor local celebrity after losing 100 pounds, but still no one would call her wispy.[31] Add in her curly red hair and she's easy to spot in a crowd. One of the cookies had broken in transit from apartment to van, and she offered it to me. It was very peanut buttery, not too sweet, and the chunks of chocolate got warm and melted in the sun. It seemed logical that we'd start hanging out together.

Claire had already more or less established her basic cookie recipe when I arrived on the scene. She began recipe development as a teen, as part of eliminating refined sugars from her diet, replacing them with substitutes like maple syrup or agave nectar. The desserts without

---

31 How does someone who is a professional cookie baker lose 100 pounds? In Claire's words, "I ate less and exercised more."

refined sugar that she found in stores tasted to her like "sawdust" or sometimes "wallpaper paste"—although to be fair to the health foods of Berkeley, where Claire grew up, she has not actually tasted wallpaper paste to verify her claims. She resents the implication that she would set out to make something vegan then settle on a subpar cookie because it's "good enough" for something without eggs, butter, or milk, because her baking career began as a protest against this kind of thinking—the many companies out there that she felt had decided subpar desserts were good enough for something without refined sugar. She bakes delicious cookies, period.

Claire based her first commercial cookie on recipes she'd designed while at Oberlin College, where she majored in computer science. The process resembled the flavor matching trial and error from last chapter, but with more careful note-taking, running experiments with the sort of structured, analytical thinking she used for the computer science. In her chocolate chip cookies, Claire began with the premise of replacing white sugar with maple syrup. She finds that the flavor of maple syrup complements the flavor of spelt flour, bringing out nuttiness and vanilla notes. So, she added spelt. It's also easier to combine maple syrup with oil than with a solid fat like butter, starting her down the path towards vegan. Claire believes that if a cookie tastes as good vegan as it does non-vegan, then she should err on the side of vegan. Beyond the fact that she doesn't want to deny vegans access to cookies, the vegan ingredients she uses don't take up refrigerator space (unlike dairy or eggs). Claire now had a vegan cookie with an alternative sugar and an alternative grain, meaning the cookie would probably attract alternative-minded customers—the type of customers who would also look for organic and local ingredients. So she found local and organic ingredients to finish the list.

Claire's recipe development lies between a home cook preparing to her own preferences and Moskowitz's statistics-based experiments. Sometimes Claire modifies her recipes in ways that go against her own preferences, if she thinks the majority of her customers will prefer the result. While she prefers a very crispy cookie, most people prefer soft, so she changed the texture. I find her cookies crisp as they are; I can only imagine what would happen if she made them to her own taste. She doesn't like nuts in her desserts, but she can recognize why other people enjoy them, so some of her products contain nuts. Claire as a businesswoman gives more deference to other people's opinion than she would when baking in her own home. At the same time, she won't let the folks who turn their noses up at a vegan product shape her final recipes, because she's baking for a particular market segment that they might not belong to. She also isn't baking for customers who prioritize finding the cheapest cookie or who won't buy cookies that look healthy (the maple syrup and spelt flour give her cookies a dark brown color that often signals "health food"). She may convert some of those groups with her cookies, but if she doesn't then she's not going to branch out into new versions to satisfy them.

I gained a small insight into the lot of the recipe developer when Claire got married. She wanted a distinctive wedding cake recipe. She took inspiration from a basic spice cake, but not with the normal spices of cinnamon and ginger; instead she used a blend of fennel, fenugreek, nutmeg, and cardamom. Plus the maple syrup. I sampled versions with different flours, with coconut milk, with cacao nibs and lemon curd filling, with cream cheese frosting and then chocolate ganache and then back to cream cheese, this time covered in shaggy shredded coconut and pumpkin seeds. Then, of course, she had to practice scaling up to wedding cake size and assembling that giant cake. At the wedding rehearsal dinner, she had several two-gallon tubs filled with wedding cake crumbs from layers that had suffered catastrophic structural failure.

I managed Claire's Farmers' Market booth on the morning before her wedding. She'd baked two cakes so she could have a backup on hand during the decorating phase. After she'd finished assembling the final cake, she sent the extra layers to the market so that I could give them away as free samples.

Many people simply enjoyed the cake. More people than I would have predicted gave advice.

"I wouldn't use this frosting; it's not vegan."

"Well, the bride isn't vegan."

"But some of her customers are."

Or . . .

"Is Claire coming out with a gluten-free version?"

"This cake is for her wedding ... today ... there are no more versions."

Or ...

"I'd have made it chocolate."

I'm a home cook who doesn't even want to take advice from the chef who wrote the recipe I'm supposedly following. For me, these sorts of customer interactions feel hopelessly frustrating. For Claire, they help her business. They're the test market. Customers' casual opinions aren't definitive, but they're important, and the opportunity for customers to have these conversations adds to the sense of artisan foods being only one step removed from what a friend would create in her home kitchen. Claire also considers this part of recipe development the most fun. When she gets a recipe that everyone agrees tastes the way it should, she enters into the much more frustrating world of bringing it from kitchen to commercial. She is keenly aware of how different ethylene packaging controls moisture differently and what she needs to wrap around cookies versus scones versus truffles. Claire knows which high-moisture fruits lower the shelf life of her scones too much for retail stores. She's learned that using a commercial mixer for her granolas breaks up the oats, so that the open edge of the grains absorbs too much liquid and ruins the texture.

Although logistical difficulties like broken oats or moldy raspberries may be frustrating, Butterfly Bakery has options for dealing with them that are peculiar to a very small-scale operation. Claire could buy different granola equipment (a small cement mixer would work) or go back to tossing the ingredients by hand. Home cooks would only have the hand mixing option; large manufacturers only have the equipment solution. Claire went with a return to mixing by hand. Similarly, for scones with high-moisture fruit, Claire could switch to dryer ingredients or sell scones with whatever fruits she likes in the Farmers' Market only, where you don't need to factor in time for shipping and sitting on a shelf. She's undecided about her scone future, but she knows she has options. That freedom to prioritize having the desired flavor over having the desired shelf life is an advantage of artisanal production.

Claire brings a particular flavor proposition to her customers. Her products reach a much smaller market than what's reached by Entenmanns's Danishes, Chips Ahoy Cookies, or Little Debbie Snack Cakes, and she's focused on understanding what *that* market can't find from conventional food manufacturers. You can see the results of deciding to target similarly niche markets in other food businesses. Artisan cheese makers, for example, often have very soft cheeses, very stinky cheeses, very sharp cheeses, very goat-y cheese—essentially cheeses that intensify different cheese attributes instead of trying to mellow them to appeal to more people. That's in contrast to the cheese-y powder in Kraft Macaroni and Cheese or on certain Wheat Thins or the red-orange cheese in a ball on cracker trays at holidays. Makers of super stinky cheeses know that fewer people will enjoy their cheese than enjoy the cheese ball, but that small, stinky-cheese-loving crowd will be tremendously happy to have the option.

Businesses like Butterfly Bakery benefit from having similar businesses nearby. If you add together all the artisan cookie bakers in Vermont, any one person surveying the cookie scene will likely find at least one variation that tastes just right. If you've only got Butterfly's cookies, one small group of customers will be fully satisfied, a second group will start off skeptical and grow to like Claire's cookie style, and a third group will decide that "artisan cookies" just aren't for them. That third group wouldn't be left cookie-less; they still have homemade cookies and standard supermarket brands available.

In theory all these forms of production fit together just fine with home cooks experimenting to suit their desires, many different artisan producers working alongside each other to cater to small groups of customers, and national food companies that put out products to reach the broadest possible customer base. Sometimes a home cook will develop her recipe into a business, sometimes an artisan business grows to become large scale—it's a fluid system. The problem is that the system has fallen badly out of balance around the "artisan" designation. The word "artisan" now stands in for all sorts of food expectations about quality and taste and wholesomeness. This term isn't regulated. No one is going to force Wheat Thins to roll out each cracker sheet by hand to earn the right to call them artisan. Furthermore, when Wheat Thins puts "artisan" in the name of a product that looks like the original, tastes a lot like the original, and costs about the same as the original (suggesting that nobody is shredding actual artisan cheese that sells for $20 a pound into the cracker dough), they simply mean to imply it's of higher quality than the next closest competitor. They don't expect to be taken literally. Artisan here serves as a marketing term that represents in one tidy word a whole bundle of positive feelings.

As much as it annoys some of us to see the word "artisan" bandied about with no real meaning, this label isn't like a nutrition label where I need someone else to determine things like how much B-12 I get from one serving because I don't have a laboratory to test it myself. In the vast majority of cases, we can perform our own test, because an artisan product tastes different from a mass-produced product, and both taste different from what would come out of your own kitchen. We're still talking different from, not better than. While Wheat Thins sit pretty high up on my preference list, some of my friends would go to any one of several local artisan bakers that sell crackers, and I don't know about your cracker-baking skills, but my homemade crackers, with all due modesty, taste delicious. The important thing is to try out foods produced at different scales of operation and pay attention to the differences in *flavor* not in marketing.

We could, if we wanted to, create a regulated artisan label that conveys additional information I couldn't get by tasting. The international Fair Trade designation does exactly this, inspecting coffee, cocoa, and other companies for compliance with rules around labor practices and governance. We could inspect, for example, the degree of "handmade" in artisan, but if most people seek out certain flavor qualities in "artisan," then most people have their own means of inspection, too. The next chapter looks at one place where the lines between differences we taste and differences we read about get truly blurry: local foods.

CHAPTER SIX

LOCAL FOODS AND
FLAVOR COMPROMISES

I DIDN'T TASTE my first store-bought green pea until I was fifteen. I'd had the *opportunity* to eat green peas from a store before then, but I wasn't the sort of kid to help myself to green peas without my mother watching, and if my mother had any involvement in a meal, it meant homegrown peas. Her vegetable garden filled our backyard. It provided our fresh vegetables during the summer; freezing or canning the harvest got us through winter. My father commented once, while observing a pea shelling session that looked like it might last all night, that she needn't feel *obligated* to put up an entire winter's worth of peas; we could just go to the grocery store.

"You say that, but you don't remember what store-bought peas taste like," my mother answered.

She was right.

I have trouble separating the flavor of peas fresh from the garden— or even frozen from the garden—from the context of how I grew up with them. For me, vegetables constitute a whole experience, not just a dish at dinner. The flavor of fresh garden peas makes me think of bright green, of pressing seeds directly into the cold spring soil after the snow melted, of the thin white flower petals and the corkscrew tendrils, the pop of opening their shells, the feel of running my thumb down the center to spill the peas out, plinking into a metal mixing bowl. Green peas are sweet, they call out for fresh milk and mint, they can become brassy if they stay on the vine too long. They make me think of June. For me, local vegetables get tangled into decades of memories, and the attitude factor of flavor comes across complex and satisfying.

Even with my vast green pea eating experience, the first time I ate a store-bought pea, I didn't know it was a pea. I served myself what *looked* like little beans from the salad bar at school. I was expecting a bean flavor and hearty texture and instead got a mouthful of mush that tasted like I'd licked the inside of a tin can. I reported the spoilage of the salad bar beans to the kitchen and received the reply that I'd taken green peas, not beans. I was shocked. Green peas? They barely qualified as gray peas. I'd had fresh peas; I'd had frozen peas; I'd had all sorts of pea preparations, but they never tasted anything like these. The local and not-local versions of the same vegetable so little resembled each other that I had no clue what I'd put on my plate.

I might be an atypical case. Still, you could say that my childhood impression of pea flavor was more correct than others' because I formed it through experiencing a type of food production—kitchen gardens—that maximizes full pea flavor. Foods' flavors change as they move further out from the backyard garden into the national, then global, food system. For a variety of reasons, which we'll get to, these changes almost always reduce the original flavor. We'll accept that flavor reduction in exchange for other benefits, like food that's available fresh year-round, food that's inexpensive, and food that includes bananas. Vermont's kitchen gardens are notably lacking in bananas. I start every morning by taking advantage of a ready supply of non-local bananas that probably taste lousy to someone from Ecuador. We all make flavor compromises.

In my family, we did not and do not eat a tomato from a grocery store in Vermont in January. I might concede, as a grown woman no longer living in my parents' house, to having store-bought peas in my freezer, but a store-bought tomato is entirely unacceptable. It is so unacceptable, in fact, that my mother built her own greenhouse attached to the dining room so that she could have fresh-picked tomatoes throughout the year. She has standards. Those standards don't allow for trucked-in tomatoes that at best have no taste and at worst taste like cardboard with an edge of bitter. The mealy, dried-out, pale tomato flesh does not signal "tomato" to her, or me, and given that they're tasteless I'd argue they shouldn't signal "tomato" to anyone.

It is indisputable that the tomato flavor intensity changes between long-distance tomatoes and local, in-season tomatoes. That doesn't mean everyone has the same preference. One former culinary instructor who I asked about this issue told the story of students spitting out a nice beefsteak tomato he brought in from his backyard garden because they found its flavor too intense. Other people respond to their first fresh local tomato ecstatically, as if it were a life-changing revelation, which, for some, it might be. In either case the eaters are reacting to a more flavorful vegetable.

I understand how tomatoes would reach this state of flavor and non-flavor. My mother only has herself to think of. After she meets her own tomato needs, she'll share with her family, then with friends and neighbors, but her main obligation is to herself. Conventional tomato farmers answer to many more expectations.[32] Consumers expect enough tomatoes to be available to meet everyone's needs—from the supermarket shopper to the pizza sauce maker to the salad bar manager. We expect fresh tomatoes throughout the year. We expect tomatoes to look good, cost a reasonable amount, and last a while on our counters after we pick them up on a weekly grocery run. Tomato farmers need to figure out production, harvesting, distribution, payments, and regulatory compliance. Just like the producers of Wheat Thins compared to the home cook, these farmers run a business, not a hobby.

The modern, commercial tomato's flavor problems begin with the need to control its ripening. As the tomato ripens on the vine, its sugars develop, its meaty and juicy texture develops, the aroma develops— basically it begins to taste like a tomato. However, as it ripens it also gets more fragile and closer to the dangerous overripe zone. The last thing a storeowner wants is a shelf full of rotten tomatoes. Or a shelf full of squished tomatoes. Or a shelf without *any* tomatoes because he couldn't ship them in from places where tomatoes grow in January. The simplest solution is for farmers to pick the tomatoes green, after they're "mature" but before they get to the fragile, squishable

---

32 "Conventional" here means the farmers who supply the majority of tomatoes we find the marketplace. Just like in the previous chapter, there are also tomato farmers equivalent to artisan producers who follow a different business structure, who we'll get to later.

(and tasty) red stage, and ship them that way. Even tomatoes labeled "vine-ripened" can leave the vine as soon as the faintest blush of red appears.

So, the sturdy green unflavorful tomatoes fan out in trucks across the country. They arrive at warehouses, distribution centers, supermarket storage rooms, and supermarket shelves relatively unscathed. We don't see lots of green tomatoes on those supermarket shelves, however, which is a shame since I have some great green tomato recipes. Tomatoes are a type of fruit that can ripen off the plant. They will ripen slowly as they're shipped, then treatment with ethylene can jumpstart the final ripening process. Plants like tomatoes produce ethylene gas naturally. It signals that it's time to get ripe; it's why unripe fruit ripens more quickly alongside ripe, ethylene-releasing fruit. Exposure to synthetic ethylene gas can also give those green tomatoes a signal to turn red. They go through a second ripening, but without the rest of the plant providing nourishment to help them develop the aromas and sugars that create flavor.

Farmers can control tomato ripening and transportability further through breeding different tomato varieties. The decisions farmers make about which tomatoes to plant have shaped this fruit for millennia. For a long time, humans have selected tastier tomatoes. The tomato's wild ancestors started as hard, sour berries, but as they evolved and humans nudged this evolution by selecting plants closer to what we wanted to eat, tomatoes became the juicy, sweet fruits growing today. As Michael Pollan noted in his book *Botany of Desire*, deliciousness became a survival of the fittest issue—if you were a plant and humans liked the way you tasted, they went out of their way to make sure you survived and had offspring. We became adept at plant breeding. Not only farmers, but also institutions like universities focused on understanding plant genetics and drawing out more desirable characteristics in new generations. Flavor, however, isn't always a priority in this process. Even at the very beginning of agriculture, you still wanted plants that were vigorous and had higher yields. Modern farmers benefit from high-yielding tomato varieties that have disease resistance, pest resistance, drought tolerance, and the ability to look perfect and travel long distances. These benefits, too, came with a flavor price.

We've known that flavor has ranked as one attribute among many when farmers choose what plants to carry on into new generations. It turns out that for tomatoes, we didn't just pass over a more flavorful tomato if a sturdier option happened to be available—we selected directly *against* flavor. We've based successful modern tomato lines on a genetic mutation that led to round fruits that ripened evenly and had uniform red color. What we didn't know at the time was that the same mutation also reduced tomatoes' sugars and nutrients. Plant breeders were propagating an anti-flavor gene. It was an unintended consequence of what seemed like good production practices.[33]

Home gardeners, who already have the advantage of eating their tomatoes at the peak of ripeness, can select tomato varieties intended for home, not commercial, use. These varieties' lineage still doesn't prioritize flavor over all else; home gardeners also like disease-resistance and drought-tolerance and other advantages that help the plants stay alive. However, flavor usually has a higher rank in the priority system. Often these plants have an "heirloom" designation. Heirloom is not an official term; in this context it means a tomato (or other plant) holdover from the age of backyard gardens, when cosmetics and transportability didn't matter as much. These tomatoes have names like Brandywine, Mountain Princess, Black Krim, and Cherokee Purple. They can look ugly, definitely not perfect round globes with an even red bloom across them, and can be fragile, but they have the full tomato flavor. Without going too far into botany, these tomatoes are open pollinated, with seeds that can be saved for next year's crop—allowing them to be passed from generation to generation and allowing ambitious home growers to experiment with their own plant breeding projects if they're so inclined.

Between global supplies of unripe tomatoes with flawless skin and backyard varieties that gardeners find most tasty stretches the gray area of "local" food. Technically, local is measured in miles not in flavors. In Vermont if you use the term "local" without specifying a

---

33 We discovered this because Cornell has a research team dedicated to understanding ripeness and flavor in tomatoes. They're at the Boyce Thompson Institute and led by James Giovannoni. You can read more about them here: http://bti.cornell.edu.

point of origin, then it means from somewhere within 30 miles of the state borders.[34] Those miles can indirectly lead to flavor improvement. Moving a shorter distance can let tomatoes (and other vegetables) get picked riper and reach consumers faster. The tomato does still require transport, however, and may need to spend a while on the shelf before anyone purchases it. Customers may or may not expect it to look like the non-local tomatoes. Growers may or may not have selected the most flavorful (and more delicate) varieties. They have options, but knowing the miles the tomato or other item traveled doesn't necessarily tell us which option they chose.

Some local farmers have increased the lines of communication and reduced some of their lingering logistical flavor challenges through what are called "direct to customer sales." In Farmers' Markets and farm stands, for example, farmers interact with shoppers without any intermediaries. There is no waiting period on store shelves. A farmer going to a Farmers' Market can pick tomatoes that morning and know they'll be in customers' kitchens by the afternoon. Plus, they have a conversation to explain things like why heirloom tomatoes look different than supermarket tomatoes or why they caution shoppers to use the tomato right away because it is at peak ripeness. Some people will argue that even these delays reduce produce's flavor; tomatoes are best picked in the sun and eaten immediately. A few farmers have eliminated *that* obstacle, too, selling shares of their harvest to subscribers who can come to the farm to pick their fill from the fields, not even stopping for a weight and price check before munching on the goods.

Tomatoes, green peas, and all the other produce represent only one segment of local food. Local food covers maple syrup and honey, poultry and beef, eggs and milk, grains, dried beans ... and we still lump these foods together into the catchall "local" category. If one flavor claim unites these disparate foods, it's the flavor of "fresh." Ask people who believe that local food tastes better to explain what sets it apart, and nine times out of ten they'll explain that it tastes fresher—even

---

34 At the time of this writing. Also, not every state regulates this term, but often foods advertised as "local" have a point of origin listed—look for it.

cheese that has aged for months in a cave, even beef wtih "dry aged" printed right on the label.

If we measure fresh by how long it takes for a food to get from where it was growing to where we're eating it, then local foods certainly have a greater chance of being fresh than the non-local competition. It's not guaranteed. The journey from farm to kitchen table may wind through stints in warehouses, storage rooms, and grocery store shelves that reduce the freshness no matter how many total miles the item traveled. The consumer needs to use food promptly, too. If I load up over-enthusiastically at the Farmers' Market, food eaten at the tail end of that supply may not offer much in the way of freshness (but at least I know who is to blame). Nonetheless, the system that brings us local food offers many freshly picked opportunities, from the beefsteak tomatoes at a farmers market to pick-your-own strawberries to corn with a "just picked" sign in a roadside farm stand.

The label "fresh" does have a legal definition in the food world. This definition does not always reflect the informal understanding of fresh to be a variation on "freshly picked." For produce, the U.S. Department of Agriculture defines fresh as food that's unprocessed or minimally processed; pre-sliced apples still count as fresh, but frozen slices do not. Unprocessed fruits and vegetables can only sit on a shelf so long before they go bad, so in that sense the legal term reflects the colloquial definition of fresh, but I'd never describe the flavor of a limp head of weeks-old, unprocessed lettuce as "fresh." In other foods the rules move even further from common understanding. Fresh chicken, for example, is not recently dispatched chicken but rather chicken that has never been frozen below 26-degrees Fahrenheit. On the other hand, fresh eggs remain in their shells. None of these rules guarantees a quick journey from farm to plate.

Official labels can be confusing, but so can our own understanding of what we're looking for. I have an "I'll know it when I taste it" attitude towards foods like green peas, for which I have decades of straight-from-the-garden experience. And I know fresh baked bread from stale, but would I know the difference between bread baked with fresh wheat and not-fresh wheat? Maybe if the wheat flour were rancid. How about root crops like potatoes and winter squash, which will eventually go bad, but not for some time after picking? Or, we could consider pre-serving food at the peak of freshness. Say I process and freeze toma-toes at their prime ripeness in August. If, in winter, I make them into pasta sauce alongside a sauce made from un-processed fresh tomatoes purchased at the supermarket, the first sauce will taste "fresh"er (more like summer) than the sauce made from the supermarket produce.

I asked a farmer in my neighborhood, Joe Buley, about these flavor issues. Joe worked as a chef before he became a farmer and served as a chef-instructor at the New England Culinary Institute. He's the one who brought students around to appreciating heirloom tomatoes straight from the garden. I figured he knew fresh flavor better than anyone else.

It was late autumn when I visited Joe. We stood at his open green-houses in a field where the grass had turned brown in an earlier, now dissipated, cold spell. Inside, spinach grew. One greenhouse's long, narrow beds had carpets of spinach coming close to maturity, and we walked in to inspect. The leaves were dark green and thick. When this spinach matured further, assuming the weather returned to cold, it would taste very sweet, as the plant bumped up its sugar levels for pro-tection against oncoming winter. Joe would pick it and bring it directly to the winter Farmers' Market in town. However, he would have trou-ble convincing his Farmers' Market customers to see this straight-from-the-greenhouse spinach as fresh, because the dark, brittle leaves wouldn't *appear* fresh. "Turgid" he said to describe the leaves—I had to admit, it didn't sound good.

If you get past the turgidity, winter spinach tastes great. Sometimes it's sweet enough to munch on by the handful as a mid-afternoon snack without feeling painfully virtuous. When faced with snackable spinach, I don't waste much time on worrying about fresh or not fresh; I rejoice, but "freshness" in appearance as well as taste has become *de rigueur* for selling local foods. And the legal definition of unprocessed isn't on many people's minds at the local Farmers' Market, either. Joe would have to explain himself and his turgid spinach to his customers.

"Fresh is a marketing term," Joe said in a resigned tone.

Joe's farm abounds with examples of freshness contradictions. He has chickens in a coop on one patch of the farm. He throws the birds food scraps, they peck around and eat the local bugs, and he has customers dedicated to his fresh chicken eggs, all of them recently laid, all of them reflecting the flavors of the pasture. Conventional eggs in supermarkets will also say "fresh." These eggs haven't been powdered, pre-pasteurized, turned into liquid, separated into yolks and whites, or anything else that would qualify them as a non-fresh product in the eyes of the government. They have expiration dates. Nonetheless, many have a lifelessness marked by long stints in refrigeration under fluorescent lights; their pale yellow yolks next to Joe's eggs' robust, marigold-orange ones are a symptom of flavor ennui. Some of their not-fresh taste is due to time and storage, some to how the chickens were raised. Either way, in spite of the promising "fresh" label, Joe would never cook with those other eggs. He's a chef—he should know.

In case I don't have an intuitive understanding of egg flavor, he gave me another example—some convenience stores have signs that say "Coffee Brewed Every 30 Minutes," and people believe that means it's fresh. I thought back to the Coffee Lab beans that, even at their best, smelled and tasted like dusty dirt roads and faded hay. Brewed in the last 30 minutes wouldn't do much for those beans. Letting them sit in storage, waiting for their 30-minute brewing wouldn't improve matters.

Joe also knows how products can lose what remains of their fresh flavor due to human error. He's concerned that some people bring delicate produce home then refrigerate it below 52 degrees, some people buy Brussels sprouts harvested from regions that don't experience that sugar-concentrating frost, and, unforgivably, many people pre-slice tomatoes, for salad bars, sandwich making, taco toppings—it is never okay. He describes pre-slicing as if he can actually see the aroma molecules seeping out and dispersing into the air before anyone can catch them. The flavor that results? Not fresh.

On the other hand, Joe holds out a fundamental hope.

"Inherently, people know," he says. "They may not be able to explain, but somewhere in our DNA after thousands of years of evolving, we know what's good and what isn't."

As with everything else, we need to explore, taste, and pay attention.

Even though most people identify fresh as the flavor of local, I'd say that the greater unifying factor is our positive attitude. The people selling or promoting local foods enthusiastically embrace this facet of flavor. It's why my local natural food store plasters the wall with posters of photogenic farm families and adorable lambs (best not to ask where the lambs end up). It's why we have agri-tourism, so tourists can associate real Vermont maple syrup with that time they went on a lovely ski vacation. It's why I opened this chapter with childhood memories; I buy into the nostalgia part of the local foods ethos. My actual childhood occurred in the 1980s, and there are limits to how nostalgic one can feel about the foods of the 1980s, so I also subscribe to the greater nostalgia for an unspecified "earlier time" when the countryside was filled with prosperous farms, wholesome living, and great-tasting tomatoes. Logically, I know that I wouldn't have appreciated those historic households' limited menu (especially in deepest winter) and that they faced serious food problems (like hunger and malnutrition), but that's what makes it nostalgia—it's not logical.

Along with nostalgia, local food rides on a sense of patriotism. Here in Vermont we believe we can produce all the food we need because we are Vermonters, and Vermont is a great nation. Conversations between either side of the producer/consumer line always end in a familiar way:

"Of *course* this town can have local kiwis/emu/wine/hops for beer/ sunflower oil/trout farms/rice paddies—we can do anything if we try."

Then, no matter how many decades it takes, a dedicated believer in the power of local will make it happen. And it's not this way only in Vermont. America as a country thinks of itself in terms of beautiful amber waves of grain, not to mention the equally beautiful fruited plain. We take pride in food production.

Close to ten years ago, Vermonters decided they wanted in on the "amber waves of grain" bit, and farmers, along with customers, began a push for more wheat production. It's hard to find much space for waves of anything in hilly Vermont, and our damp climate isn't conducive to grain production, either. Some farms were growing wheat anyhow, which often went to animal feed. The ultimate goal was flour and, eventually, a truly local bread. Bread, after all, is a staple food, and it seemed only right that we become self-sufficient in its production.

For a short time in the eighteenth and nineteenth centuries, Vermont *had* grown and milled a credible amount of wheat—before the West became more accessible, with its flat, dry fields that are much more hospitable to growing grains. The pro-Vermont flour lobby used this history as proof that we could do it again, and a well-respected local bakery signed on to the project.

It turns out that it takes more than just bringing in a wheat crop to make flour that passes muster at a commercial bakery. The farmers experimenting with wheat had been referring to agronomic indicators to guide them, measurements like yield and resources required to reach that yield, not the wheat's final performance in artisan bread. A baker partner could now test bakery performance, but a fair test required precise data on the flour. For example, the bakers needed to know its moisture content to control the rising process and texture of the final loaf. Getting this information required laboratory testing. Once farmers had test results from the lab and the bakery, they could adjust their wheat varieties and growing practices to improve the final flour, which took another round of research, experimentation and time.[35] In the interim, to procure an early version of the all-local bread, you needed to know someone who knew someone who would pick the loaves up from a nighttime drop point. Each loaf came with a full page of disclaimer notes explaining why the loaf *was not* up to the bakery's quality standards and why you should under no circumstances tell anyone what bakery produced it. If you tried to re-sell one of these loaves, I believe they promised to come after your firstborn child.

I knew someone who knew someone, so I sampled some of the first batch allowed beyond the bakery walls. It tasted fine to me. Perhaps a tad dense. As I gnawed on it, I felt like a pioneer—a local food pioneer supporting a future of wheat abundance by consuming bread that embarrassed its baker to the point of hiding. I felt proud.

The next step in the bread's evolving salability drew on Community Supported Agriculture (CSA). In a pure CSA, customers pre-purchase a "share" of a farm's crop to be delivered on a set schedule (usually

---

35 For a play-by-play of how this development process works, you can read all about it from the University of Vermont's grains project: http://www.uvm.edu/extension /cropsoil.

weekly) during the growing season. Farmers get their payment before production, the time it's most needed for supplies and other expenses, and the subscribers assume the risk of a poor growing year or the prospects of a banner year. Many CSAs have evolved to be closer to a grocery subscription service, with a variety of local products aggregated by one farm (or other business). The captive CSA subscribers, who have essentially raised their hands and declared, "I support local food, *a lot*," can become a testing ground for new products added onto their regular shares—the local orchard making pies from their apples, cheese makers trying out a new style of cheese, sunflower oil freshly pressed from the local sunflower harvest. The early all-local loaves, still wrapped in warning labels, arrived in the CSAs next.

Now, a lot of agronomy work was going on, with wheat breeding, trial crops raised for disease resistance, and a laboratory that could test for something called a falling number that bakers need to know, while I the consumer had joined my neighbors in hacking off pieces of still-in-development bread and rooting for the home team. I supported local bread by eating it and saying nice things about it in the same spirit that I might have grown a beard to support the 2013 Red Sox, if I'd had a beard to grow.

Then, a few years after those first experimental loaves, I arrived at the bakery itself and saw success: bread loaves with crisp crusts and airy insides and no warning labels. It was our very own, all-local, Cyrus Pringle bread, named for a Vermont wheat breeder from the 1800s. It technically tasted like the bakery's other breads—that had been, after all, the goal—but to those Vermonters who believed in our wheat farmers, who had stuck around for the development process, it tasted like the best, most brilliant bread anyone had ever invented. It tasted like pure genius.

Just because a food is a basic need doesn't mean it has some immutable taste that stays the same across every sample. Even setting aside the highly subjective attitude element of food, differences exist, even where we're accustomed to seeing ingredients as interchangeable. If I said my house was the blue one on the street, you would know which house I meant, just like you could pick out "green peas" from a plateful of carrots. If I asked you to *paint* my house blue, you would need a lot more information about the particular shade I had in mind. A recipe may call for peas, but "pea" encompasses many different flavor options like "blue" encompasses different color options.

The 1896 *Fannie Farmer Boston Cooking School Cookbook*, part of an early generation of books meant to teach cooking, notes of peas:

> They appear in market as early as April, coming from Florida and California, and although high in price are hardly worth buying, they having been picked so long. Native peas may be obtained the middle of June, and last until the first of September. The early June are small peas contained in a small pod. McLean, the best peas, are small peas in large flat pods. Champion peas are large, and the pods are well-filled, but they lack sweetness. Marrowfat peas are the largest in the market and are usually sweet.

Most modern cookbooks merely write "peas" and occasionally offer instruction for substituting frozen for fresh. Not every cookbook follows this convention. Deborah Madison, in *Vegetable Literacy*, provides an introduction to fresh peas that reminds the home cook that "there are hundreds of varieties of peas. Jefferson alone grew thirty varieties in his gardens at Monticello." She provides a sentence for a few of her favorites: Golden Sweet, Green Arrow, Tom Thumb, Lincoln, Corne de Belier, Champion of England, and Canoe. Madison targets the home gardener or at least Farmers' Market connoisseur. On the other end, *Cook's Country Cookbook* assumes a supermarket shopper as its audience and warns against buying fresh peas, because by the time they get home it will be too late, their sugars turned to starch and the texture mealy. Instead, this book calibrates its recipes to frozen green peas and names the brands they used.

Home cooks experimenting with ingredients will develop their own instincts. I stopped buying fresh supermarket peas long before *Cook's Country* warned me off. If I want fresh peas, I'll pick and eat them from a backyard garden for a bright flavor. I toss frozen peas into thick pasta sauces because they add color and a texture that can stand alongside the pasta, and the flavor is pleasant but not dominating. I would not drown my mother's backyard garden peas in sauce unless I was using a recipe developed by someone who knew how to set off, not hide, their particular flavor. If I hadn't grown up with backyard food-centered meals, I don't know that I would have internalized these distinctions. I don't trust my instincts to know how to use grassfed meat or eggs from heritage breeds of chicken, ingredients that I did not grow up with in my backyard. Maybe one day, with enough practice and instruction, I will.

The shorthand of green pea (or tomato or spinach or eggs) glosses over the details of exactly what flavor we have in mind. This shorthand makes sense or we'd never get through a grocery list, but we should realize that it's a shorthand. Understanding the difference that "local" makes in flavor requires us to go deeper into the details of what distinguishes one green pea from another, one tomato from another, and so on. Simply noting miles traveled doesn't cover the bases. It's complicated; I won't lie. It asks us to think about the larger food system and about how the decisions other people make shape the flavors available to us. I believe the flavor rewards far outweigh the time it takes to navigate these waters, and besides, I enjoy navigating them. Getting complicated here simply means no one will run out of things to learn any time soon ... and that's what keeps our eating life interesting.

CHAPTER SEVEN

NEXT STEPS:
THE WHERES AND WHYS OF FLAVOR

SUPPOSE THAT YOU eat a potato for dinner. You've harvested it directly from your backyard. It tastes as fresh as a potato can taste, a just-dug fingerling with delicate skin and buttery flavor. It's local. But does it taste like your backyard? Does it taste like your town? Your state? Suppose that you live in Idaho or Maine, two famous potato states. Would you take a bite and say, "Now that's a fine example of a potato from Boise"?

The last chapter started with defining local in miles traveled, but we could instead define local as tasting like a particular place, food that carries a local *character* regardless of where it may travel. Think of it this way: I can pick up and move to Paris tomorrow, and I'd be located in Paris, but I'd hardly qualify as a *Parisienne*—I'd still be a Vermonter. The people in France would say it works the same way for a fine wine—a Champagne that arrives in Vermont carries the character of the Champagne region of France. If I wanted a truly local food experience, by this reasoning, I'd go to Champagne (the place) and drink Champagne (the wine) in its hometown. Second best would be to invite the taste of Champagne (the place) into my Vermont dining room by purchasing Champagne (the wine).

This type of place-based flavor often goes by the French name *terroir*, translated in English as taste of place.[36] Other countries, primarily in Europe, have processes for understanding taste of place and labeling this sort of flavor to communicate it to customers. If the factors involved in understanding the flavor of "fresh" or labeling for "artisan"

---

36 The book *Taste of Place* by Amy Trubek explores this whole concept in detail.

seemed complicated in the previous chapters, that's nothing compared to taste of place. Pliny wrote about the regional character of wines in ancient Rome, and the term *terroir* (if not its label) shows up in agricultural treatises dating back at least to the 1600s. The modern system started with French winemakers from Bordeaux and from Champagne in the early twentieth century.[37] It has expanded to include many other products since then, but we'll stick with French wine for the moment to sketch out the basics of how this all works.

Multiple factors shape a wine's flavor. A certain number of these factors connect to place of origin, for example the soil types and the microclimates of the vineyards where grapes grew. The variety of grape changes wine flavor, and also connects to place because some grapes grow better in different climates and soils. Even the human element of production connects to place, because the traditions of a particular place shape winemaking practices. These traditions will cover everything from pruning the vines and managing the yields, to how the pressing is done, how long a wine remains on its lees (the sediment in the barrel), and what sort of barrels the wine ages in. For Champagne you also have the method of secondary fermentation and riddling (rotating lees to the neck of the bottle) used to create the bubbles. A protocol exists outlining all the factors, from the soil up, that qualify a wine as a Champagne. They contain quality standards embedded in them but go beyond quality to describe uniqueness. Because this uniqueness relies on the environment and tradition of a particular region, one could say that Champagne tastes like Champagne. Other sparkling wines might taste great and be of high quality—the Cavas of Spain and Proseccos of Italy, for example—but they don't taste exactly like a French Champagne.

Turning observations of what can constitute taste of place into an official label takes some doing. First, you need to begin with a food product that's established within a region. Then you need to demonstrate that specific factors in that region shape the flavor of the food. You need to document the exact processes for making the food—recording those steps that, if changed, would also change the flavor. After you document these, any producer who meets the location

---

37 Again, see *Taste of Place* by Amy Trubek for details.

requirement and production requirements can apply for a label verifying that they produce a true Champagne or whatever the product may be. Setting up this system requires the work of many experts—agronomists, soil scientists, sociologists, geologists, botanists, historians. It requires tasting panels to verify the scientists' and winemakers' theories about how flavor changes when the place changes. Then on top of that you add a governing body to enforce it all.

This system takes a lot of work and money to set up—but consider it from the perspective of the French winemakers who took part in its creation. They created wines, Bordeaux and Champagne, that had gained an international reputation. This reputation, and an accompanying price premium, created an incentive for winemakers in other places to label their sparkling wines "Champagne" as well. These outside producers didn't have the same soil and climate, possibly not even the same grapes, as the regional producers. Even for those inside the Champagne region, as businesses grew and financial stresses appeared, it could become appealing to cut a few corners here and there—letting the wine age a little less time, dropping the time-consuming riddling process, and so on. These changes would affect the character of the wine. Even if they only altered it a little at first, added up over time and across producers, they could change the character considerably. These possibilities don't even include outright fraud, slapping a Champagne label on lower quality wines with the intent of duping customers.

Winemakers didn't propose that Champagne have a monopoly on sparkling white wines—it doesn't—but—they did want to make sure that a traditional Champagne remained a traditional Champagne and customers knew what they were getting. By making an official record of how one creates a Champagne, they could offer a guide for future winemakers while also verifying for customers what they're buying. It's preserving local tradition, but it's also good business sense, protecting generations of winemakers' territory in the premium wine market.

I admit that I don't know my Prosecco from my Cava from my Champagne from my sparkling white California wine. However, I do respect the right of people who *can* tell the difference to get the wine they're after, and the right of winemakers to produce their traditional wines without fear of food forgery. The same taste of place framework applies to non-wine items; cheeses, cured meats, olives and olive oil, and spirits, for example, have gained similar official recognition. The general term for labeling products based on place is "geographical indication." You might see this label as *appellation de origine controlee* (AOC) on French products, or Protected Designation of Origin (PDO) on other European products. Canada introduced the first North American equivalent to the European system with their designation of Charlevoix Lamb in 2009. The United States does not have an equivalent system.

The closest the U.S. currently comes to the European system for designating taste of place is the certification mark. Certification marks mean a product has met an approved set of standards to receive whatever the "mark" may be. So, for example, the Idaho Potato Commission has a certification mark that indicates whether a potato is in fact from Idaho and meets Idaho quality standards—making it an Idaho® potato.[38] It's a sort of trademark, except that other trademarks you can buy once and keep; they do not require re-certification. If I purchase rights to the Nike Swoosh symbol, then I've got the Swoosh and can use it within whatever parameters the contract sets out. I don't need to *earn* my Swoosh rights each year. Idaho® potato farmers need to pass regular inspections to meet Idaho Potato Commission standards, and they'll lose their labeling rights if they fail. In addition, the potato farmers using this certification mark don't own it; they simply use it to show they've met another organization's standards while that organization controls the mark.

Agricultural policy makers debate whether a group could adopt European-style taste of place standards and enforce them via certification mark. One problem would be communicating the differences between interpretations of geographical indicators. If Idaho kept its current system, which says a potato came from Idaho but nothing about traditional varieties or particular soils or tasting different than a Maine potato, while Maine went for a "taste of place" potato labeling system, it would take a whole lot of explaining which label meant what. It adds a new layer of complication to a concept that's already

---

38 http://www.idahopotato.com—a site with a lot of information.

confusing. A certain number of customers need to buy (literally) into the idea to be able to pay for the experts, inspectors, and enforcement behind a meaningful label and to incentivize farmers to go through the bother. To get those customers you add marketers and communications experts into the cost, plus lawyers, plus international trade negotiators, plus the food and agronomy experts ... it becomes not only complicated but also expensive.

A few years ago, Vermont started looking into whether a geographical labeling system in the spirit of French wine might work for maple syrup. Maple is, after all, a traditional Vermont product. It has a relatively complex flavor that some believe derives its nuances from place-related factors. An existing state-regulated grading system separates maple into different grades based on color, clarity, sugar content, and importantly taste. This delineation means that not only do we recognize natural changes to the flavor of the syrup (for example, as the season gets warmer) but we also have inspectors trained to taste maple syrup to check for compliance with existing regulations. They don't currently taste for *terroir*-type nuances; the grading taste descriptors deal in relatively broad brushstrokes, concerned mostly with intensity. However, they become very familiar with maple flavor along the way, and as we saw in the complex flavors chapter, familiarity goes a long way towards catching nuance. Plus, frameworks for identifying the more subtle maple flavors do exist. Quebec has developed a maple syrup flavor wheel similar to the ones in coffee and wine, with flavor note possibilities that include roasted dandelion root, juniper, and cloves. The University of Vermont offers a pared-down version, with flavors like vanilla, crème brulee, and nutmeg. It might be possible to build a *terroir* of maple from the foundation of an existing system.

When I worked at Vermont's Agency of Agriculture, my personal maple goal was to maneuver my way onto a maple syrup tasting panel... without having to go through the full training used for real inspectors. I started early pleading my case to Henry Marckres, head of the maple division and perhaps the best maple taster in the world.

Henry pointed out to me that, while I might have visions of Champagne, his maple syrup tasting focused on catching off flavors

(flavors that don't belong in maple syrup) and helping sugarers learn what these flavors teach them about flaws in their production. For example, even a little bit too much safflower oil or cream used to defoam the boiling sap carries through into the syrup. Letting sap wait too long before boiling can mean a sour taste like orange juice starting to turn. Not all off flavors taste unpleasant or at least not to all tasters. Collecting sap from trees after they've budded leads to "buddy" flavor. Henry describes buddy as "like a Tootsie Roll," and I know some back-yard sugarers who intentionally make their syrup a little buddy to get that Tootsie taste. To me, buddy tastes like a ripe kitchen compost pail smells—sweet and decaying. I support keeping buddy syrup out of the marketplace even if some people like it. Henry also experiments with creating off flavors, like with a decades-old syrup he's using to track the progress of absorbing the metallic taste of old tin. I dutifully tasted the off flavors. I made disgusted faces. And Henry eventually agreed that I could tag along for judging syrups at the annual St. Albans Maple Festival.

The day before the festival began, we judges convened in a science classroom at the local high school. Every table and countertop held unmarked glass jars of syrup, plastic spoons, and hydrometers for measuring sugar content. I grabbed a spoon and leapt straight into the tasting.

One thing became immediately apparent—no one should ever re-use containers for storing syrup. Syrup picks up all sorts of flavors you don't realize remain in a jar. I tasted peanut butter, pickles, toma-toes, bacon grease, salsa, bubble gum, and ham. I also discovered that I have a much lower sugar consumption capacity than I'd imagined.[39] After fifteen minutes of taste panel duty, I was raiding the supper the Women's Club had prepared for us to eat when we'd finished—I was desperate for food to offset the sugar. Henry can go for hours without pause. His record is 932 samples, approximately half a gallon of syrup, consumed in one day. Most relevant to the project at hand, I learned that maple syrups taste different even after separating by grade and disqualifying the off flavors. We agreed unanimously on the winner—a very dark syrup with a maple taste so clear that you forgot you were

---

39 Unlike wine tasters, syrup tasters don't spit after they sip—it's hard to spit syrup.

drinking sugar. It tasted correct for its grade, but it didn't taste like the others alongside it. The intensity of the dark grade didn't muddle the maple flavor. The sweetness was as balanced as a maple syrup could hope to be. I would have sipped it after dinner like a cordial.

If maple syrup is able to reflect place in the way that Champagne does, then you would expect to find this *terroir* in contests like the one in St. Albans. Many entries come from small farms and amateur sugarers who would use sap from a particular area, rather than larger operations that might blend saps and syrups from many locations. Tasting happens within a grade, so holds constant for any flavor changes that might happen across a grade rather than across a place.[40] The people judging the samples usually have judged lots of syrup before, building that maple familiarity and perhaps picking up on nuances others would miss.

Truly testing for the effects of place on maple syrup flavor would require modifications to the typical syrup judging method. Researchers investigating the possibility of *terroir* need to show not only that syrups taste different, but also why. They record what sugarbush (stand of maple trees used in sugaring) syrups come from and make note of its characteristics, like soil type. They disqualify syrups that blend sap from distinctly different soils into one syrup. Also, although making syrup is pretty straightforward—you put sap in an evaporator pan and boil off the water until it's syrup—some technical differences exist, like using a reverse osmosis filter to remove water before boiling. In this instance, reverse osmosis would eliminate a sample from the group because the study needs to hold the technology constant just like it holds grade constant. You would also need a better way to verify that tasters aren't imagining the difference. A three-sample test, which the team investigating maple *terroir* used, presents two samples from one source, one from another, all unmarked. The hope is to reliably identify the odd one out then link that to place-based factors.

In some tests the syrups taste too similar to get the right answer consistently across tasters and over time. Sometimes the differences are remarkable; some syrups taste spicy, cinnamony, floral, and even

---

40 The same trees will produce different grades of syrup within the same sugaring season; those flavor differences come from changes in the trees themselves, not from change in location.

soapy (a natural soapiness, not due to a poor rinsing job after cleaning the tank). One sugarer in Thetford has a stand that produces syrup with a distinct red tinge that tastes like vanilla. These observations suggest that even if not all environmental changes change flavor (the indistinguishable samples) some do. We can take observed variation in maple flavor, add in the traditions built around syrup's production and the institutional infrastructure of research and trained maple tasters, and see a path towards place-based syrup designations like the designations employed by French winemakers. Except, we don't have a rule for what makes syrup flavor change between locations. Without understanding that mechanism, it's not possible to write up a set of guidelines that tell a producer—if you create maple syrup in a place with these characteristics, using this particular process, you'll have a Northeast Kingdom Amber different from a Northern New Hampshire Robust. Without agreed-on guidelines, formal labeling can't move forward.

People exploring taste of place, either the fully vetted and labeled variety, like Champagne, or the loose observations of local characteristics, like maple syrup, all subscribe to one broad perspective: relying on nature's variability and imperfections to generate serendipitous flavors. We may stop there or add some human craft elements to riff on the non-standard flavors we stumble upon. The bubbles of Champagne, for example, began as a mistake that winemakers first tried to correct, then embraced, and finally immortalized in their rulemaking.

Sometimes the most interesting flavors emerge from a process very different than building off of whatever chance elements nature throws our way. Some chefs utilize extreme precision (often with the help of inventive kitchen equipment) and a detailed scientific understanding of why food behaves the way it does, combined with their own *avant garde* ideas about what food could be. Their perspectives take the science and technology other chefs and food producers regularly employ, then pushes them a few steps further towards the point where science meets science fiction, resulting in a unique new cuisine.

At one level the movement to bring more and better science into the kitchen simply gives a fact check to the kitchen truisms that have built up through centuries of informal experimenting. At some point, though, it crosses a line into new culinary feats that form their own canon of cooking technique. Some chefs call this "molecular gastronomy"; others claim molecular gastronomy is just the science part, that when you add chef-y artistic sensibility you need a new term like "modernist cuisine." We'll stick with molecular gastronomy. While the staples of the traditional American diet are plain, simple foods like meatloaf and mashed potatoes, the staples of molecular gastronomy lean towards the spectacular. The further chefs can push both the science and the art, the better. If you line up a centrifuge, Anti-Griddle (which reduces food instantly to minus-thirty degrees Fahrenheit), rotary evaporator, dehydrator, spray dryer (turns anything into a dry powder), lasers, and other laboratory equipment, you can create such dishes as mozzarella balloons filled with tomato foam, a spring (the Slinky kind) made from olive oil served in a jewelry box of salt, and a cocktail made of laser-vaporized orange and wine.[41]

The techniques behind these menu items combine advanced organic chemistry with the detail craftwork one might use to produce a Faberge egg. Add in the equipment costs and you end up with something most of us wouldn't try at home. In 2011, Nathan Myhrvold, a former Microsoft executive whose kitchen is, in fact, a large laboratory, published a six-volume cookbook called *Modernist Cuisine*. It promised to unlock the secrets of scientific cooking for anyone with $625 (the listed price on Amazon), the patience to read 2,500 pages, and enough equipment to outfit a hospital. While this book can seem ridiculous to an average amateur chef (as compared to, say, a billionaire eccentric genius amateur chef like Myhrvold), it made an important point—the world lacked a comprehensive, up-to-date investigation into the science of cooking.

The link between kitchen laboratory and average kitchen isn't as weak as it might first appear. Other authors had written about kitchen science before, but it's a pretty recent phenomenon. Harold McGee, in the introduction to the 2004 edition of his *On Food and Cooking*,

---

41 From the menus of Alinea, El Bulli, and Moto, respectively.

noted that when he published the first edition in 1984, cooking was a discipline separate from biology or chemistry, with few people combining them. Myhrvold goes further than McGee, beyond how science explains familiar foods and cooking, into what is possible, especially with the assistance of new gadgets like ultrasonic baths or custom-made grills for emulsifying large wedges of cheese.[42] His starting point is similar, however. When Myhrvold and his co-authors, Chris Young and Maxime Bilet, announced on their website that they'd won the prestigious James Beard Award for Cookbook of the Year (2012), they began with a Beard quote: "Too few people understand a really good sandwich." They wanted to understand the sandwich and everything else.

Myhrvold offers fundamentally graspable examples to explain *Modernist Cuisine*. One example is pea butter, which results when a centrifuge separates green pea puree into juice, starch, and a thin layer of bright green fat—the butter. That makes sense; breaking down a pea into its component parts then taking the fatty bit as your butter. It requires a large quantity of peas to collect enough butter for one piece of toast, but if you're going to go to the trouble of investing in a centrifuge, what's a few extra dollars for the peas to put in it?

Unfortunately, while laypeople might understand the pea butter concept, most of us lack the equipment to try our hand at the technique. To move the science and technology back one step further to what we can not only understand but also create in the average kitchen, we might turn to Hervé This. This, a French chemist, first coined the term "molecular gastronomy." His recipes run the gamut from elaborate dishes for advanced chefs to projects for children. Science, including kitchen science, encompasses all levels of education. Mix baking soda and vinegar to make a mini-volcano—that's kitchen science. He even works with the French ministry of education to develop workshops for primary school classrooms.

You can see This's pragmatic side in his two-ingredient chocolate mousse. Take your favorite high quality chocolate bar, melt it down

---

42 *Popular Science* magazine posted a gallery of equipment highlights ahead of the publication of Modernist Cuisine. It's available online at http://www.popsci.com /technology/article/2011-02/tour-modernist-cuisine-kitchen-laboratory.

with water in a ratio of 8 ounces chocolate to 6 ounces water, then whisk vigorously as it cools over an ice bath.[43] It sets up like a very airy mousse or, more accurately, a Chantilly. Voilá, you've created a gourmet dessert.

The principle behind this technique is roughly the same as whipped cream. Whipped cream consists of buttery fat plus water (aka "cream") whisked vigorously until it thickens. The butter and fat arrive in our kitchen already combined in the form of cream, so we need only dump a carton of that cream into a bowl for whipping. For the mousse, we accomplish essentially the same thing as whipping cream, except with the additional step of first combining the fat (sugary fat in the form of chocolate) and water by melting them together to produce a single liquid. Then, whip the air in and keep it cool to keep it stable. You can get into colloids and emulsion classifications versus foams and stabilizing with fat versus protein, if you want to delve further into the science. I didn't want to delve into the science; I did want to delve into the chocolate.

I did careful research on the candy bar I most wanted to transform into mousse and landed on Laughing Moon Chocolate from Stowe, Vermont. It took some minor math to figure out the ratio of chocolate to water, and some major arm exercise to whip the melted chocolate and water into the proper mousse-ness ... but it worked. I'd had no expectation of success when I'd started out.

Lawrence was away on a business trip at the time and I called him immediately to share my triumph.

"It's brilliant!" I gushed. "If I ever need to impress a date, this is the dessert."

"You don't need to impress me," Lawrence said. "And I don't like desserts."

"Not you, then—some other date. And if I need to pair it with something, I think I'd definitely go with a cigar. And an aged tequila. I've never been into tequila before, but it seems right."

---

43 For more detailed instructions, I recommend the *Washington Post*'s retelling of the original recipe, published Feb. 13th, 2008 as "Chocolate Chantilly" online at http://www.washingtonpost.com.

"Why don't you make me some chocolate mousse when I get home," Lawrence said. "I'll be impressed."

I agreed.

Kitchen science doesn't complete the molecular gastronomy picture, because it still needs the *avant garde* art sensibility. A two-ingredient mousse, while a neat trick, doesn't have the same flair as a giant manmade puffball, which, when scooped into the mouth, collapses into the essence of popcorn (from El Bulli). That sort of dish takes both a higher level of science and an unconventional artistic instinct. However, as unconventional as the thinking may be, it's still grounded in the senses that make up flavor, the same ones that provided our basic flavor vocabulary. We can still work backwards to guess at the thinking process that some enterprising soul might follow to get from the simple mousse to creating dessert out of sea buckthorn foam, malted white chocolate, anti-griddled borage flowers, and a sprinkle of powdered jasmine nectar served alongside an ocean soundscape. Chefs playing with molecular or modernist techniques may turn the volume up to eleven, but they haven't departed for an entirely different plane of flavor experience.

Think about the visual component of flavor. Moto restaurant, in Chicago, loves elaborate visual tricks, like their "tuna" sushi rolls that look and taste like sushi, but are made from watermelon. Moto also serves its sushi rolls alongside a picture of a sushi roll printed on edible paper that tastes, yes, like the sushi roll. Sometimes their dishes look like one thing and taste like another. For example, what appears to be a plate of nachos is really dessert—with substitutions like mango sorbet shredded into liquid nitrogen and frozen in the shape of shredded cheese.[44] Because skilled chefs design these contrasts between visual expectations and actual taste, I assume they achieve a more pleasing effect than when I pop a red jelly bean into my mouth thinking it's cherry only to discover that it's cinnamon. I do know how to make the potluck pleaser of a meatloaf cooked in a cake pan and frosted with whipped mashed potatoes so that it looks like dessert. I

44 You can find both these examples in a TED talk by Homaro Contu and Ben Roche from March, 2011 at http://www.ted.com.

once had garlic granola (tastes similar to Chex Mix) with chip dip ice cream that looked like your typical parfait but didn't taste that way. It was pretty good.

Texture is another popular variable, like "caviar" that's really Iberian ham and melon formed into little spheroids, or salt foams on top of margaritas, or carbonated grapes. Of course, unusual texture created excitement long before any modernist cuisine. Pop rocks were a seminal contribution to the oeuvre, along with Dippin' Dots and the tingly British sherbet powder that traces its roots back to medieval times. I would argue that the giant popcorn puffball is derivative of my favorite childhood kitchen stunt—putting hot chocolate with a large marshmallow in the microwave and seeing how far the marshmallow can puff out before exploding.

Then there's aroma. We already know that aroma provides the lion's share of what we experience as flavor. Aromas can act as ingredients in their own right. Some dishes involve burning a bed of hay, rosemary, or autumn leaves upon serving. Moto offers a dessert called "smell the glove" (it's a *Spinal Tap* reference) that requires deep inhalation of leather scent. More commonly, some restaurants bring out a bowl with a generous dollop of green sauce and a sprinkling of tiny herb snippets, then add hot water to form a steaming soup right below your nose. I'm a sucker for that trick; catching the very first burst of the soup's aroma makes me feel pampered in a way that sets the mood for the rest of the meal.

I gave the aroma-as-ingredient concept more thought on a second visit to Eric Svensson at the Coffee Lab. He'd just received a shipment of new Dunkin' Donuts flavors, including cinnamon roll.

"Can I smell it?" I asked.

Eric handed the bag over.

I inhaled.

"Smells like the inside of a Dunkin' Donuts," I said. You could smell both the coffee and the warm pastries in that bag of grounds. Interestingly, it did *not* smell like a Cinnabon or any other place selling coffee and cinnamon rolls. Proprietary cinnamon roll scents? A touch of jelly doughnut aroma added in? I inhaled again. I imagined myself as a dieter attempting to get enough satisfaction from the smell that

I didn't feel a need to consume actual calories. How would this smell translate into a taste? I pictured myself lapping at the air of a doughnut shop.

"I could make you a cup," Eric said, breaking my reverie.

The coffee tasted stale. Eric pointed out that the developers had calibrated it for serving with sugar and cream. I added those. Now it *did* taste like something familiar, like the half coffee-half French vanilla flavored hot chocolate concoctions I'd made at gas stations when I was in college. They kept me awake. "Bubbaccinos," Eric called them. I hadn't had one in years. I paused for momentary remembrance of the college years, then I went back to sniffing the grounds.

The people working on Dunkin' Donuts coffee are some of the best in the business at engineering aromas. Plus, they're plying their trade in a beverage where everyone knows that the aroma makes the drink. The ritual of enjoying a cup of coffee begins with an instinctive long, deep breath above a steaming mug. We also know that coffee aroma inspires artists as well as chemists. Visit the popular Coffee Review website, and you enter a poetic place where the natural aroma found in a cup conveys both black sage and white sage, night-blooming flowers and dusk blooming flower, and "complex flowers running from honeysuckle to lavender."[45] I don't know which flowers fall between honeysuckle and lavender in the order of things, but I imagine orange blossoms might and perhaps lilac, definitely neither geraniums nor carnations. Eric warned me that these descriptions, while lovely, were neither accurate nor replicable.

"But what if," I asked him, setting my Dunkin' Cinnamon Roll blend aside, "What if this writer is someone who really does live in a world where coffee smells like resin and dusk flowers? If it's real to him… I don't know, then that's kind of great, right? I would like to live that way."

Creating new ways of experiencing the world seems to lie at the heart of many a gastronomic manipulation. After all, isn't it often our intent to give someone a new perspective on the world through food— understanding a piece of our childhood through them eating the foods

45 http://www.coffeereview.com

we ate or virtually visiting our hometown by recreating local cuisine? And, taking it a step further, don't we expect each generation to have artists who lend us a vision that is radically different? Sometimes the artists providing those new perspectives are chefs, and sometimes they use the tools of science to make their vision come alive.

Perhaps not everyone can create a world-changing dining experience, but the idea of inventing a flavor no one has tasted before holds undeniable appeal. Between debuting at Alinea and adding flavors together to come up with a palatable dinner, there's much to explore. Stepping into that terrain tempts both rock star chefs and kitchen putterers like me. I'm not looking to do anything extravagant—no vaporized orange—but I'd like to come up at least with something unexpected.

During one of my bouts of feeling that I really *ought* to get more aggressive in trying to create new flavors, my friend Claire (the cookie baker) received a magazine assignment to invent new cocktails that included maple syrup. She sent me a text message that I should pack up all the possible mixers in my kitchen and come over to her place for a recipe development session. It was perfect. What better place to find new flavors than in cocktails—the drinks where anything from pine-infused vodka to rose petals to a Mezcal worm is welcome?

Creating cocktails is as close as most of us come to dabbling in alchemy. In a cocktail, you might have the sensation of drinking an entire floral arrangement, or an herb garden, or all of a tree from leaves to bark to root. Cocktails bring us exotic flavors through lemongrass, sugarcane, sloe plums, the secret Trinidadian spices in Angostura bitters, the bitter orange peels in a Creole shrub. Cocktails have a certain Sir Walter Scott romance, built from spirits aged for decades in casks in guarded cellars. Or maybe it's more of a Humphrey Bogart romance—I served an entire Moroccan feast on my front lawn as an excuse to imbibe in Champagne cocktails, the drink of choice in *Casablanca*. Cocktails have ceremony. Lawrence sips mint juleps from a silver cup on Kentucky Derby Day. On Christmas Eve, my parents and their friends finish the holiday meal with homemade cordials in thimble-like glasses. I guess there's a fairytale element, too—not just the thimble glasses, but I haven't forgotten that Alice drank cordials to grow bigger and smaller in *Wonderland*. Surely I could invent something new playing around with cocktails.

In response to Claire's invitation, I got out a large cardboard box and filled it with honey, a lime, an orange, Rose's lime syrup, bitters (Angostura, Blood Orange, Dandelion), cream, buttermilk, raw eggs, beer, coffee, juice spritzers, tonic, seltzer, hot sauces, white peach balsamic vinegar, red wine that had turned to vinegar, bacon, gourmet cocoa powder, tea, olive juice (I'd already eaten the olives), and jalapenos.

I arrived at Claire's house, dropped my box on the small dining table beside a kitchen counter she'd already covered with her own ingredients, and headed downstairs to her alcohol shrine.

The shrine is really a large entertainment set in Claire's basement. It's filled with all sorts of liquors collected from small distilleries across the U.S. and Canada, plus a lineup of tasting glasses for sampling. At the beginning or end of a dinner party Claire will invite her guests to visit the booze, and we'll troop down the stairs to sip from each bottle until we decide what suits our mood that evening. Usually the answer is Noah's Mill Bourbon, occasionally Ungava Gin from Canada or an Ice Apple Crème Liqueur from Boyden Winery in Vermont. Claire spins this basement feature as a sign of frugality, because she and her husband worked out a modest monthly entertainment allowance and stocked the entertainment center entirely from that line in the household budget. And a post-dinner cocktail has fewer calories than other desserts. Very sensible. The night of the cocktail invention party, we returned from the basement unfrugally with armfuls of bottles.

Surveying a kitchen stocked with possible ingredients and a cocktail shaker that seemed inadequate to the taste ahead, I asked Claire to elaborate on her recipe development process.

"Mix stuff together, then taste it," she said. I knew that strategy. I had practiced that strategy. This time, however, with so many possible ingredients arrayed before me, the number of potential combinations felt overwhelming.

I once took recipe development baking classes that Claire taught. We started with a base recipe, say for vanilla cake, then spent two hours working our way through variations, answering questions like how the cake changed with different types of flour—combinations of barley, spelt, whole wheat, rice, rye, buckwheat, cornmeal. Partly we learned the properties of each flour; mostly we learned to feel okay about failure, to admit when something we concocted tasted lousy and move on. I tried to get back into that mindset with the cocktails.

Claire pointed out that mixing drinks offers several advantages over baking cakes for the trial and error approach. For one thing, you can scale them down very small without messing up the chemistry—making a quarter cup of cake batter wouldn't accomplish much but a few ounces of cocktail works fine. You don't have to wait for them to bake—just mix, sip, adjust, mix, sip, and so on. Our palates also accept far more possible flavors in cocktails than in cakes. Plenty of candy-sweet cocktails exist. Very rarely do you find a bitter cake—Claire in fact had made cakes seasoned with bitter quinine bark in an attempt to develop a gin and tonic cake, to no avail.

Claire narrated more thoughts on flavors while she mixed. "Licorice and celery are flavors that open my taste buds," she said, "and I feel flavors in different places in my mouth and look for ones that round each other out. Like, if I'm making a mustard, onion is a supporting flavor, vinegar is on the side, then I need something with the mustard seeds to complete the top … like coriander." She set about searching through the mixers for well-rounded combinations.

Lacking my own internal framework for building rounded flavors, I started to mix at random. I began to understand how the Long Island Iced Tea may have come about, as I layered one ingredient on top of another on top of another, hoping that the next addition might rescue the mélange. A coffee, red wine, maple syrup combination, with orange bitters, then lemon juice, finally got tossed when a cream liqueur (on the theory that you put cream in coffee) turned it pink but failed to save it.

"Vomit," Claire identified the flavor of another attempt. "If you combine whiskey, gin, maple syrup, and pickle juice, it will taste like vomit," making it neither a likeable flavor nor a new one. Claire still hadn't given up on maple and pickle juice themed drinks. She believed that with perseverance we could mimic the classic sugar-on-snow combination of Vermont maple syrup, raised doughnut, and a pickle. I started to point out that if it were possible, some hip Vermont bartender would have done it by now, but she'd already moved from that idea to the idea of frying up bacon to use as a swizzle stick. The more cocktail experiments we conducted, the more we struggled to focus on any single line of culinary inquiry.

I wouldn't say that we broke new ground in drink recipes. Successful creativity requires more than one evening of alcohol. As Claire later summarized in her article, most of our attempts suggested that maple syrup should stick to its day job—covering pancakes and waffles.[46] If I'd studied my molecular gastronomy before heading out, we might have rallied by adding new texture to old standbys—floating maple spheroids in a Sidecar or powdering Ice Apple Crème Liquor to sprinkle over mulled wine. In the absence of those options, we ended the evening pouring large measures of local whiskey over maple ice cream and eating it with a chaser of bacon. It's hard to go wrong with liquor on ice cream. It's hard to go wrong with bacon. I called Lawrence to drive me home.

Eventually, I'm going to come up with that brand new flavor. Hervé This probably comes up with a dozen before breakfast; surely I can manage a few of my own in the course of a lifetime. I may not have had moments of brilliance with the cocktails, but I learned some new things. As a variation on a Shandy, we came up with a beer and mead mixture that really, really called out for a carbonated grape, which in turn inspired me to learn grape carbonation. Claire and I began to see the point of spices on the rims of glasses—it's not just for margaritas. We particularly liked adding some heat with cinnamon or sweetness with maple sugar. I'll never be shy about using bacon as a swizzle stick. Not groundbreaking, but new ideas will lead to more new ideas until some day I intend to work my way out into the realm of true innovation. Will creating something new mean I really understand flavor? Maybe. If nothing else, it means I've been exploring it and making my own discoveries along the way.

---

46 "Set the Table with Maple Mixed Drinks" in the Spring, 2013 issue of Vermont's Local Banquet.

CHAPTER EIGHT

DISCOVERING FLAVOR

THERE'S A SEASONING that makes food taste wild—like the green of pea tendrils, the rawness of maple sap dripping from the thawing tree, the edge where a cucumber's flesh meets the dark green skin, the smell of pumpkin vines growing riotously across a field. I first tasted this flavor in a sweet miso salad dressing, served over micro-greens snipped by a very patient person from indoor trays in the dead of winter. I'd never tasted anything like it before.

The problem with this particular flavor is that it happens to come from ground silkworm pupae. Yes, bugs. That means I can't get it from the spice section at my local grocery store. And it's probably not coming to my local grocery store any time soon, because I don't see a huge local demand for ground-up bugs to sprinkle in food. I see demand for fruit fly catchers and sticky papers to keep bugs *out* of food, but few are clamoring to add them in. I also don't know how to raise and process my own silkworms, nor do I particularly care to learn. I first tasted the pupae as part of a bug-eating dinner held at Nutty Steph's (home of the bacon, chocolate, and wine Thursdays) organized by a local woman on a mission to convert more people to using bugs as ingredients.

I did not love every bug at the dinner. Gnocchi and pancakes made with cricket flour got two thumbs up; the bugs added a new flavor dimension similar to the salad dressing. The dried mealworms in chocolate hazelnut truffles added a crackly texture that lightened a super-dense chocolate but not as much as crisped rice would have. The pan-fried crickets, which we ate in generous pinches like trail mix, tasted like gamy vegetables to me. To be fair to the crickets, plenty of foods work best as one of many ingredients—for example, in flour, but not when eaten in isolation. I'm not going to suck on a cinnamon stick or crunch whole peppercorns, either. And I've only tasted the crickets once; eight more tries and I might come around. Lawrence really enjoyed them.

The people who hosted the dinner offered many arguments for why Americans should eat bugs. I'd read about these ideas before. To begin with, most cultures *do* eat and enjoy bugs. A friend of mine still craves the Mopane worms that she and everyone else ate as a bar snack in Namibia. I know several people with the habit of nibbling on ants (they taste lemony). It's weird here, but not other places. Furthermore, bugs offer a source of protein that's easy to farm, requiring only modest amounts of resources, and no less an august body than the United Nations has declared them to be the most important food of the future.[47] I understand their point. I agree, until the arguments end, as they inevitably do, with a nutritional comparison between a hamburger and the cricket equivalent. Crickets offer lots more protein on a per-100-gram basis, but I can't get my taste buds on board with a hamburger-sized patty of squashed insects. A hamburger with a silkworm aioli? That I'd order in an instant, which doesn't do much for resource conservation but certainly would do a lot for my dining pleasure.

In bugs we see the delicate balance between over-thinking and under-thinking our food that can get us in trouble us when it comes to flavor exploration. On the under-thinking side, I'd simply never thought about how to use bugs in a recipe. I'd heard the rational arguments for eating bugs. I'd wondered if I would get a chance to taste one and, if I did, whether I could handle what I imagined as a squishy bug gut texture.[48] I never thought about enjoying them or chefs using them for flavor more than for novelty, an oversight that I now recognize as an error.

The over-thinking comes with dwelling on the fact that these dishes contain bugs. That's when our cultural bias towards disgust kicks in, and it's unfair because most of us are adept at switching off that sort of over-thinking when it comes time to eat. Perhaps some people sit down to a bowl of ice cream and can't get past what milk

---

47 From "Edible Insects"," a 2013 report by the United Nations Food and Agriculture Organization.

48 I feel like I should point out that in addition to the fact that powdered bugs clearly don't have an unpleasant texture, even the fat whole pupae didn't have the texture I'd expected—it's more like the texture of potatoes.

is: a white secretion from a cow's mammary glands. Maybe other people drizzle honey across a hot biscuit and picture bee vomit. I do not. There's a reason why we have a saying about not wanting to watch the sausage get made. We also don't discuss at the dinner table how digestion works. Our society has all sorts of buffers built up around over-thinking, which allow us to set squeamishness aside and just eat our food. I did not need to (and in fact did not) picture the entomological ingredients behind the gnocchi, pancakes, salad dressing, and truffles.

For a long time, I prided myself in my under-thinking/over-thinking balance. After all, I'm someone who can enjoy a bug dinner. I ate rotted shark and did not ask why it tasted like blue cheese. I could guess, but I left that thought alone. I've also done my part to think through where I can find new flavors, I've even attempted to learn wine appreciation and I drank some of the buddiest maple syrup ever produced.[49] Soon after the bugs, though, I began to notice all the ways that I was not as aware of or even open to the flavors around me as I liked to believe.

The first sign came from my friend Chaya. When I was growing up, Chaya had been my best friend. Her house was a five-mile bike ride away, up a snaking back road, on a property with sunny fields, its own water wheel, a mill pond with dark cold water, and a little sandy beach in the bend of a meandering stream where the water dropped just deep enough to make a serviceable swimming hole. Recently, she sent me a posting of her old house, up for sale again. The owner's pitch concluded:

> One thing I will miss ... is the crayfish. These are miniature lobsters, which are abundant in the mill pond and downstream. I made a little trap in which I put bacon or dog food. I tie a rope to it and toss it into the pond. Come back 24 hours later and its full

---

49 It was intentionally made that way as a way to torture Henry Marckres. It tasted like the time, in college, when I took a dare to eat a plate where some guys had mushed together a spoonful of everything from the cafeteria dinner line (which included a taco bar, pudding bar, and leftover Froot Loops from breakfast) then poured tequila over the top. Exactly like that.

of them. Put them into a pot of boiling water and you can have yourself quite a feed. They are tiny compared to lobsters, but I think they taste even better.

A crayfish feed? I distinctly remembered my parents telling me that the crayfish in Chaya's pond weren't edible. Chaya and I had brewed dandelions into bitter tea, munched on sweet clover, collected rosehips, didn't particularly enjoy the taste of any of it, and the whole time I believed the crayfish didn't have anything to offer. Making traps, baiting traps, waiting 24 hours, then building a fire on the beach, cooking, and eating—that would have provided at least a weekend's worth of entertainment. I tried to convince Lawrence that we should buy the property and have mini-lobster bakes all through the summer, but he wouldn't agree to the plan.

Soon after the crayfish revelation, I heard a local radio program about eating invasive species in which I learned that I'd also been misled about the edibility of Zebra mussels.

Next, I learned from one cookbook that lupines—which I knew only as purple, white, occasionally yellow, wildflowers—have edible seeds, lupini beans. I'd been eating these disinterestedly as part of a gourmet olive mix for years without realizing what they were. Then, I read in another cookbook about sautéing milkweed pods in butter as a side dish for a summer supper. I asked my friends, what flowers would be next? I already knew about day lilies, Johnny Jump Ups, and dandelions. Edible trout lilies were next, as it turned out. I love this early spring flower: bright yellow blossoms with curled back petals growing on single stalks over wide, dark green leaves, speckled like a trout belly. They blanket whole clearings in the woods, dappled in the sun, which earns them their second nickname of fawn lilies. I rode my bike to the woods one warm May morning to taste trout lilies. Their leaves have the succulence of tender spinach, with a taste that combined buttercrunch lettuce and a trace of wintergreen. Their petals offer a more delicate version of the leaves' flavor, with a tannic sweetness like just-ripened bananas.

I'm not describing any journey off to a foreign bug eating culture or local wild crafting lore I picked up over decades of exploring my surroundings. I'm describing what I learned in a few days' time, just by chatting with friends, playing the radio while making dinner, leafing through a cookbook, and being open to the ideas they presented. Even a passive curiosity can lead to uncovering new potential; actively questioning what is possible (or, at least, edible) uncovers far more. Learning new skills brings you another step further out in flavor exploration, skills like how to raise those silkworms, how to identify a true Champagne, how to pick up a few molecular gastronomy techniques. It seems endless. Except, it's not—and that's where the true consequences of both thinking too much and thinking too little reveal themselves: our choices are disappearing faster than we're exploring them.

There are many reasons why flavors disappear. The process of selecting what sort of crops our farms will grow steadily narrows the contenders as one variety becomes widely favored over another. The world lost 75 percent of crop diversity from 1900 to 2000, and the U.S. lost 90 percent over the same time. Humans once relied on 7,000 species for food; only 150 are in commercial cultivation today, and of those, 30 provide 95 percent of our calories. Certain remaining crops have fared worse than others. For example, in China only 10 percent of the 10,000 varieties of wheat grown in 1949 remain, and the U.S. has lost 95 percent of our apple diversity.[50] Meanwhile, the wild plants and ancestors to these crops face their own threats, from stresses such as habitat loss and climate change.

The animals we use for food fare poorly for some of the same reasons as the plants, farmer selection combined with environmental threats to their wild relatives. Animals also illustrate the wrinkle of human management of wild stocks. Fishing is one example. When I first met Rowan Jacobsen, the wine guy from the Complex Flavors chapter, he was finishing an article for *Yankee Magazine* (published in November 2013) on New England cod—or the lack of New England cod. Dramatically incorrect estimates in the cod population for 2007 and 2008 led the National Oceanic and Atmospheric Association (NOAA) to set fishermen's quotas far too high, leading to a collapse in

---

50 These numbers come primarily from the United Nations' Food and Agriculture Organization, and the Global Crop Diversity Trust (http://www.croptrust.org).

the fish and, after 500 years of a thriving commercial industry, the declaration, "Cod is dead." Rowan recommends switching our preferences to former "trash" fish (dogfish, monkfish) in preparation. The same scenario plays out with other species around the world.

Some foods have plenty of their ingredients still available but disappear because generations forget the skills to make them. The organization Slow Food, with chapters around the world, brings attention to these endangered traditional foods. Their Ark of Taste project, begun in 1996, documents unique foods with strong ties to a place that face a clear risk of loss. Slow Food describes an imminent threat as existing

> "... when the knowledge and skills necessary to produce a food belong to one or a few producers, mainly elderly. It is not enough to have a written recipe or simple oral explanation in order to produce a cheese, cured meat, or traditional dessert. Traditional processing methods are the work of artisans, and learning the techniques means working with them for years. One must learn the skills and acquire an indefinable but necessary sensitivity to be able to maintain constant the quality of a product even when the conditions in which the production takes place (the temperature, humidity of the places of work and aging, the time of year, the state of the animals' health, etc.) change."[51]

Slow Food's virtual Ark currently contains 1,677 products, 172 of them from the United States, including artisanal American apple brandy, Sourwood Honey and Piki Bread. They are always collecting more.[52]

Some of these problems come from failures to plan ahead, to think through consequences of agricultural decisions, to identify culinary skills in danger of being lost, to figure out effective ways to preserve food diversity or support local agriculture or just not overfish the cod. Other problems come from letting our brains get in the way of

---

51 http://slowfoodfoundation.com

52 Currently in this case means spring of 2014.

exploring tastes—rejecting food that isn't packaged attractively or well advertised, or that uses ingredients that are no longer fashionable, or that isn't part of our cultural norm but might be part of somebody else's. We've lost the appropriate balance. It's not an imbalance confined to the culinary realm, either. The diminishing flavors in our world have become a yardstick measuring other diminishments—of environmental health, of sensory connections to the world around us, of our interest in honoring other cultures and our own cultural traditions, of creativity and curiosity.

Flavor should not be a finite resource in danger of running low. Yet, even though food science has reached a level of technological wizardry that brings us to the limits of human creativity, and the number of food products introduced every year by American companies hovers around 20,000, we're primarily churning out endless variations on the simple tastes of sugar, salt, or sugar-plus-salt.[53] We've built up an ambitious diversity in packaging. We can render almost any food squeezable. Plus, we have many bright colors. But in actual flavors, we've fallen far short of our potential.

Producing unique flavor is like anything else that requires skill combined with knowledge—neglect it and the breadth of flavors we can experience is in danger of collapsing down to a very limited menu. We might decide to accept that menu. We currently appear to. Eventually, though, we reach a point where the dwindling flavor resources comes not from voluntary neglect, but from the results of that neglect leaving us with a narrow set of options for subsistence and (a personal concern of mine) enjoyment. The good news is, we encounter food and drink every day that invite us to venture outside of our known world in the spirit of exploration and discovery. We can keep active an interest in diversity and an engagement in the foods around us. A decent cup of coffee will suffice to get started. And we don't need more than an amateur's knowledge to have something to say about it.

---

53 New products estimates taken from the U.S. Department of Agriculture, Economic Research Service, http://www.ers.usda.gov/topics/food-markets-prices/processing-marketing/new-products.aspx#.UpzEz-JSJwQ Accessed January 2013.

ADDITIONAL READING

CHAPTER ONE:
IT'S NOT ABOUT WHAT YOU LIKE ...
IT'S ABOUT WHAT'S DIFFERENT

As cited in the Chapter, for a fairly detailed look at what sensory analysts and flavor experts do, refer to Barb Stuckey's 2012 book *Taste What You've Been Missing*. There are also some amusing chapters on this world in Mary Roach's 2013 book *Gulp*, covering humans tasting pet food and also rancid olive oil.

For additional information on coffee:
- Specialty Coffee Association of America (www.scaa.org)
- Sweet Maria's—Resources and information for home coffee roasters (www.sweetmarias.com)
- Coffee Review (www.coffeereview.com)

CHAPTER TWO:
BASIC VOCABULARY OF TASTE

America's Test Kitchen (www.amerciastestkitchen.com) provides a whole library of information to explore the basic vocabulary of taste. They have cookbooks, magazines (*Cook's Illustrated* was the start of their cooking media empire), videos, podcasts, websites ... some of it free and some of it requiring payment.

America's Test Kitchen describes their recipe development process in detail, and so you can see how they worked on different elements of each dish, including the balance of tastes, the texture, and the appearance. They also do taste tests which break down common foods into the components of their flavors to describe differences.

For an overview of the different attitudes we take towards food and how those shape our perception, check out Tom Vanderbilt's article "Accounting for Taste" in the June, 2013, *Smithsonian* magazine.

Maybe the best discussion about familiarity and acceptance of unusual taste came in Jeffrey Steingarten's *The Man Who Ate Everything* (1997). His book opens with a self-imposed plan of eliminating all traces of being a picky eater before he starts on his new job as food critic at *Vogue*. This plan requires him to eat at least one food he detests each day for six months—it's a regimen that turns his opinion around about foods like kimchi, clams, and lard, but fails to change his perspective on Indian desserts. "Eight Indian dinners taught me that not every Indian dessert has the texture and taste of face cream. Far from it. Some have the texture and taste of tennis balls" he reports.

CHAPTER THREE:
COMPLEX FLAVORS AND SUBTLE FLAVOR DIFFERENCES

As noted in the text, I'm not the great with the wine. The references I used most (after skimming a bunch of them):
- Richard Betts *Essential Scratch & Sniff Guide to Becoming a Wine Expert* (2013)
- Kermit Lynch *Adventures on the Wine Route* (1988)
- Rowan Jacobsen, *American Terroir* (2010), the wine chapter.

Wine writing does not have a monopoly on descriptions of subtle and complex flavors. Edward Behr's *50 Foods* offers a prime example of a writer providing a sommelier-type perspective to a range of foods.

CHAPTER FOUR: FLAVOR COMBINATIONS

While many cookbooks offer proscriptive recipes with maybe a variation or two, others focus more on creating frameworks that let home cooks find their way to new flavor combinations.

Mark Bittman's cookbooks, such as *How to Cook Everything*, take this home cook empowerment approach. For example, his pizza section begins with the basics of making pizza at home then adds in six ideas for making a more flavorful crust and sixteen quick ideas for toppings, along with more extensive recipes for less-familiar pizza variations like baked white pizza with potatoes or pissaladiere (caramelized onion spread and anchovies).

Even further on the "framework as recipe" spectrum there is the *Flavor Bible* as mentioned, as well as the *Vegetarian Flavor Bible*, both by Karen Page and Andrew Dornenburg. And, boldly, Michael Ruhlman's Ratio that summarizes all recipes as ratios (like 1 part sugar to 2 parts fat to 3 parts flour for cookies).

CHAPTER FIVE:

ARTISAN MYSTIQUE

The book *Sugar, Salt, Fat* by Michael Moss offers an investigation into how major food companies develop formulas for their products. The content is great. But I offer the book with a reservation—Moss feels a need to write some variation on "corporations are evil!" every other sentence. Maybe he's right, maybe not, either way be prepared if you're thin skinned about that sort of thing. Other insights into developing popular, national-scale food products come from Harold Moskovitz (referenced in the text) and his book *How to Sell Blue Elephants*. And there is also the previously cited *Taste What You've Been Missing*.

Candy Freak by Steve Almond may be considered an homage to the widening divide between artisan and mass produced food. In this book he tours the world of (dwindling) regional candy bar manufacturers.

For an amusing, and useful, take on homemade food compared to mass produced food, *Make the Bread, Buy the Butter* by Jennifer Reese chronicles her year of trying to reproduce common foods from scratch. It involves buying goats. This book is technically a cookbook, but you can also read it as a collection of very short essays that happen to have a recipe attached.

If you want to know what it's like to scale up from homemade to professional, but from a general curiosity perspective not a "how-to," *Delancey* by Molly Wizenberg offers a window into the process via memoir. Conveniently enough, her first memoir was focused on homemade food: *A Homemade Life*. If she goes to work for Kraft, we'll have a trifecta for scales of production.

CHAPTER SIX:
LOCAL FOODS & FLAVOR COMPROMISES

Because local food is a popular topic, you can find lots of articles on eating local under the general "food writing" heading. The annual Best Food Writing anthology is chock full of them. An entire franchise system of magazines exists to discuss local flavors, called *Edible Communities*, found online at www.ediblecommunities.com.

Many books about local food focus on political, economic, and / or environmental factors more than flavor. Some particular recommendations for looking at the changes in flavor that happen betwixt backyard and national production:

- *Plenty* by Alisa Smith and J.B. McKinnon
- "True Grits", *The New Yorker*, October 31, 2011, Burkhard Bilger's profile of chef Sean Brock (Brock also authored the cookbook *Heritage* another good, yet expensive, option)
- *Vegetable Literacy* by Deborah Madison (a cookbook)
- The Slow Food organization: www.slowfoodusa.org or www. slowfood.com
- *Omnivore's Dilemma* by Michael Pollan, which looks at many different aspects of food systems.

Much of what I include about *terroir* came from conferences and research trips from my earlier life in agricultural policy. However, two books that cover the topic as it applies to American food in detail:
- *The Taste of Place* by Amy Trubek (2008)
- The aforementioned *American Terroir* by Rowan Jacobsen.

The flavor wheel for maple syrup can be found from the Canadian Government's Agriculture and Agri-Food research at the site: http://www.agr.gc.ca/eng/

On the molecular gastronomy / modernist cuisine topic, for everyone who has hundreds of dollars to spend there is Nathan Myhrvold's tome *Modernist Cuisine* (there is a home version: *Modernist Cuisine at Home*). Also, there is a boxed set of recipe and photography books about Ferran Adria's restaurant and food laboratory ElBulli (*ElBulli 1998-2002*).

For the rest of us, here are some alternative introductions:
- "Cooking as Alchemy" Homaro Cantu and Ben Roche video on TED.com
- Herve This—it would be so much easier if we were all fluent in French, but there are English translations of some of his writing, including his book *Molecular Gastronomy: Exploring the Science of Flavor*
- It may be tongue in cheek, but one excellent introduction to cutting edge cuisine is the Gluttony chapter in Peter Sagal's *The Book of Vice*
- Although not technically describing a particular cuisine, technology meets avant garde artistic sensibility on a regular basis in the blog Edible Geography www.ediblegeography.com

Thank You ...

Multiple people helped with the research and work behind this book. Most of them are mentioned in the text. To summarize, I would like to thank: Pamela Petro (adviser extraordinaire), Lawrence Miller, Eric Svensson, Claire Fitts-Georges, Rowan Jacobsen, Suzanne Podhaizer, Gregory O'Brien, Meghan Sheridan, Carrie Abels (editor of Vermont's Local Banquet—some of the research done for this book also informed articles in her excellent magazine), Joe Buley, Jake Lahne, Amy Trubek, and Alexandra Johnson (the reviewer of the earliest versions of this manuscript when it was just a handful of stories).